ANCOATS LAD

My Parents

I was born on 23rd January 1898 at 43 Piercy Street near Ancoats Hospital. My father Harry was an Irishman and worked at Hyde Road tram shed on the electrical side, but I barely remember him as he died when I was a baby in arms. Before I was born he had been to America looking for work and he went on the bottle when he came back. He came home drunk one Christmas Eve and went to sleep on the hearth rug. Well, he'd supped so much spirits that next morning it was all over and he was found dead where he lay. Mother was left with me and my younger brother Harry, and she soon married one of my father's mates, Thomas Farrell. They had one child called Thomas who died and my stepbrother John, who is quite a bit younger than me. So we were quite a small family for the time, although there were some close relatives about who were like brothers and sisters to us, especially Arthur and Nellie.

Mother came from County Cork and knew all the old Irish songs; she was a good singer too, especially after she'd had a few drinks. She was a big, fine woman with arms on her like a blacksmith's and she worked hard all her life doing washing, office cleaning - anything. In the end she settled on street trading, selling fish out of a three-wheeled truck with skinned rabbits hanging from the handles which she pushed round Ancoats, up Ashton New Road and round Openshaw and Clayton. They called her Fish Maggie. She used to wear a neck shawl, a big shawl over that and a pair of clogs, and her hands were all twisted with rheumatism as a result of being out in the pouring rain.

She would be at Smithfield Market at five o'clock in the morning, buying Australian frozen rabbits in a big case. They cost fourpence each or three for a shilling and she would buy about forty couple. We would break the crate open at home, pull out the rabbits, which were as stiff as concrete, and hang them over a rope line in the back kitchen to thaw out. Underneath would be sheets of brown paper to catch the blood. By the next morning they would be ready and she'd skin them herself. It was my job to swill the wagon out and clean the knives and cutting boards, ready for her to use.

Most of the profit was in the skins for which you would get between eight and ten shillings. The perfect ones were then bought up by the hat factories in Denton and Stockport, where they took the fur off and used the hide to make gloves, trilbys and hard hats. The imperfect skins fetched very little - they were called wracks and were used for something else. I don't know what.

As well as the rabbits, Mother would buy a fourteen-pound box of Finnan haddock and a box of seconds kippers for about 1/3d. There would be anything from fifty to sixty pairs of kippers in a box and she'd sell them at a penny a pair. Sometimes she would let people have them on credit and call for the money at the weekend - one of my jobs as a schoolboy was to go round with my garf and hook collecting the money from those who had missed paying. I would catch

Smithfield Market from Oak Street in the 1890s

them in and say, "Me mam's sent me for the fish money," and the reply would be, "I can't give her the lot this week. I'll have to give her so much."

My mother couldn't read or write but nobody could twist her out of a penny! She kept her accounts with a piece of blue mould on the door of the cupboard where she put her groceries. When we asked what it was she'd say, "Now you go away - I know what that is. I understand it. I never went to school but I always met the scholars coming home."

She hit on another way of making money for a few years - she opened a shop in the front of the house selling ribs and cabbage and roast potatoes. She was a good cook and people would come to our house at 3 Lelia Street with their basins and plates and get a sheet of ribs or a "monkey's elbow" (a bacon pestle) for coppers. The house used to be full! Mother ordered her meat from Lovell and Christmas's bacon warehouse at Hanging Ditch and I had to go down with a two-wheeled truck the old fellow made for me to bring the ribs and pestles back.

Then the old woman took on another business as well. Frank McConville, the butcher in Fairfield Street, offered her commission if she could sell a bit of beef on the side and she agreed terms with him - she wouldn't work for nothing! She got one customer's order for weekend meat (there were few orders during the week because they couldn't pay for it) and by the time Mother had brought her order back, the woman had spread it round the neighbourhood. After that, at the weekends she'd have a table full of meat there as well as the pans on the gas stove and the fire, boiling the cabbage and ribs.

Yet another sideline came about quite by chance. Our Arthur worked at the railway chopping stores where they mixed corn and feed for the horses. He brought two fellows home one day in his dinner hour and the old woman had a big tater pie in the middle of the table for us. She filled two plates for them and said, "If you want a dinner I'll cook for you and I won't charge you much." She had four men coming for their dinner every day and after a bit they asked if she could cook them tea as well!

The only time she had off was Whit Week, when the house would be stacked with food and we all had to help ourselves. She'd say, "It's my week this week," and be on the booze all week, made up like the first lady in the land. My stepfather would go with her - he never put a suit on until Whit Week. On the Whit Friday she'd look at him and say, "You're

Piercy Street, where Mick Burke was born

not coming with me like that - not this week, anyroad. Take that off!" and he'd have to change.

Although she never made me go to church, she had an altar in the front room and would go on her knees in front of the crucifix. Father would say, "You're a bloody old fool, Maggie. There's nobody listening to you," and she'd reply, "And you're a bloody heathen!"

My stepfather was a red-hot Communist, redder than blood and when the priest came he'd argue with him: "I've seen you going to the bank at the corner of Every Street with that bag full of money. That's your God!" Mother would be furious and say, "You ought to be ashamed of yourself, Tommy. God forgive you. You're an atheist!" and he'd go on, "It's true. They own land, they own property, they own everything while poor people are starving. It's the truth and you don't like it. You'll never convert me!" Priests were always glad to get out of our house!

Despite his politics, our stepfather had been a soldier in the 5th Volunteer Battalion from Ardwick Barracks. He had time for other things, too - he was a good step dancer and floor dancer and in his younger days had danced with Dan Leno for the championship at the Cass Theatre in Mosley Street. He used to talk to us kids more than most fathers did in those days and I remember him telling about the great Philips Park flood in 1872, when the cemetery was flooded. He said the water was flowing over the top of the bridge over the Medlock on London Road and bringing the coffins with it on to the road near Tipping Street.

A great pal of my stepfather's who had the same principles was Leslie Lever. Later he was MP for Rusholme and Ardwick and Lord Mayor of Manchester. He was a solicitor by training and was nicknamed "the poor man's lawyer" because he worked from the Round House Mission on Every Street helping the poor and needy. He was a very generous man and would go round the local boozers joining in with the locals and buying drinks for them. I remember him taking two big jugs out of our house into the Blind Man's at the top of Russell Street and coming back with them filled. Another time when I was older he was with us on a trip to Morecambe and the drink on the bus had run out. He made the driver stop at a hotel, bought beer for those who went in with him and filled a big flask with whisky to share out. We thought the world about him and everywhere he went he was made welcome. He never slept - he'd be in the streets of Ancoats at eleven o'clock in the morning and he'd still be there at three or four the following morning. When we lived at 165 Every Street I've come in, thinking I was late, at twelve o'clock and he's been there, sitting on the sofa and talking to my parents about politics. Even then he would say, "I'm sorry I'm going to leave you. I've got another call yet."

Father was also a strong union man and would speak his mind no matter whom he offended. He was well informed, too - he knew all the history of the Royal Family and he knew that King Teddy was knocking about with

Fairfield Street in 1904

different women. Of course, it didn't make him very popular when he said so! I think people were more patriotic in those days and, to be candid, they didn't vote for the principle, they voted for the colour. I still know people who vote Conservative because their mother always did.

The Exchange Division, where we lived, was always Tory - I think there was only one Liberal MP, Noton Barclay. I remember Winston Churchill and his entourage coming down in their tall hats and frock coats to look at the working classes and there were lads running round the town with no shoes on their feet. It was shocking!

Schooldays

My first school was St Alban's in John Street, Ancoats. I started there at the age of five, then when we moved to Stand Street I went to St Augustine's Catholic School in Granby Row, near to the fire station on London Road. Just next door, about where the technical college on Whitworth Street stands today, was the Church of England school, with the entrance so close that you could mistake it and walk into the wrong one. When I first went we sat next to one another on long forms pulled up to long tables and with this arrangement we could peep over our neighbours' shoulders to see what they were putting down. We used both paper and slates and there were a lot of monitors' jobs - wiping the slates, cleaning the board for the teacher and so on. Later they began to install separate desks.

Many children got free lace-up clogs, which were given out by the police then - you should have heard the clatter in the classroom! The teachers used to come round and inspect your footwear when the weather was bad and they would also ask, "Whose father is out of work?" and make you stand on a form and show you up. My stepfather was out of a job then and the old woman was getting a living any way she could, so I got breakfast and dinner free at Whitworth Street School. I think this was arranged through the education authority. I remember quite well the accession of George V in 1910 when everyone got a box of chocolates with portraits of the King and Queen Mary on the lid.

The headmaster of Granby Row was Mr Littlewood and the mistress of the infants' was Miss Cruikshank. I had a teacher called Fletcher, then another called Anderson. They were very keen on your handwriting then - it all had to slope in the right direction and be thick and thin in the correct places. I liked school except for what we called "Manual" - practical lessons like woodwork - and was in the top class, Standard VII, when I left.

Most of the children were rough and ready, but very obedient. You didn't need telling twice to do anything in those days or you got a clout right away. Punishment was very severe and they could be villains with you, especially Mr Littlewood. The teacher sent me to him one day for the tawse because I had done something wrong. From our room you had to go through the middle room where he was and down the steps to the toilets. Well, I walked straight through to the toilets, wasted three or four minutes and then

Winston Churchill in Manchester in 1908

went straight back, rubbing and shaking my hands. I got away with it, too!

The School Board man was called Daddy West and he used to follow any children he came across in the streets until he eventually tracked them down. Persistent truants were sent to Mill Street Industrial School from eight in the morning until six at night. I remember that one as being like a remand home and full of bad characters but not all industrial schools were like that - often the children were just orphans or came from bad homes. They used to teach them a trade, usually tailoring or shoemaking, and there was a lot of drilling. The school at Ardwick Green had a big square at the back of it for this and the lads often went into the army when they were of age. The bandmaster there was a big, stern fellow who was a villain with them if they did anything wrong, but it was a good band. Most industrial schools had military and reed bands - St Joseph's, Stockport Road was another - and it was a pity that they were never allowed in the band contests because they always put on a good show.

I only remember being taken out of school once, to the Horsfall Museum on the corner of Every Street and afterwards we had to write about our visit. When I was a lad Ancoats Hall was a lovely building and all the schools took their pupils to the Museum, which was a fine place inside. The railway company took it over eventually and used it for their social club at the time when I was a member.

Another bit of excitement was when representatives from the Hippodrome Theatre came round. They were staging a "Water Spectacular", when the stage was removed and the area filled with water, and they were looking for good swimmers to dive into it from the boxes. I never went but the children who did were paid 7/6d a week.

There was a great emphasis on religion then and a priest called Francis Timony, known as Father Tim, came round regularly. He was a good six feet six inches tall, wore bell-bottomed trousers and a big trilby, all in black and carried a walking stick which was more like a shillelagh. He never knocked, he just walked in and if he got no answer he'd say, "I know where you are; you're hiding up the cole hole," and he'd go all over the house! We used to run off and leave the old woman to it - she was terrified of him. Later, when our Nellie got married, she used to make her lads go to St Alban's on Ancoats Lane before they had any breakfast. "Get washed and get out," she'd say. "Your breakfast will be ready when you come back." On Monday morning at school we were asked, "Did you go to Mass on Sunday? What was the service?" and if we hadn't been we would go round the playground asking the other kids, "What was on?" If the teachers found out that you'd missed Mass you would be kept behind at school until six o'clock, doing various jobs such as getting books out and cleaning up.

We used to go on Whit walks with both St Alban's and St Augustine's. People were very conscientious about walking then, especially Roman Catholics, and the grown-ups used to go too. There was a large Italian community in Manchester and they used to walk with St Michael's, George Leigh Street, which was the school most of them went to.

The Horsfall Museum on Great Ancoats Street

Then there was a Polish church on Rochdale Road with a big cellar for dancing; it was always very well patronised.

I don't remember much about the other schools in the neighbourhood except St Andrew's National School in Baird Street. From the playground on the roof there you could look down on to London Road Station and see all the activity. After the area was cleared it was taken over by Moffat's, the toffee people, but there is no trace of it today.

St Augustine's had a graveyard outside and before I left school we were off for two months while they pulled all the bodies out of the graves and reburied them in Moston cemetery. There was a low wall near where the College of Technology (UMIST) is today and wrappers were erected so that nobody could see what was going on. Of course, it was only bones coming out and they used two-wheeled box carts to transport them to Moston. The ground was left vacant for many years until they put up the UMIST building. The break suited me because I sold papers while we were off and did quite well.

The official school leaving age was fourteen but if your father was out of work your parents could apply for permission to go earlier. Mine did so and the authorities let me leave at thirteen, on 23rd January 1911.

Where I grew up

From Piercy Street we moved to Stand Street, off Store Street, Ancoats, and the area between Store Street and the arches just behind London Road Station was where I grew up. The houses were all one-up, one-down or two-up, two-down with flag floors. Our wash sink was in the street and at night we had to go to the tap outside, press a button and fill two buckets ready for morning. The toilets were "Dolly Vardens" and the nightsoil men came round to empty them at midnight on a Sunday making a hell of a row.

Nearly every night when they were shunting at the station there would be the sounds of blowing horns, capstans working and wagons banging into one another. The horns were a warning to tell the railwaymen there were wagons approaching and the capstans worked the turntables to route each wagon on to its correct line. Then the man in charge would blow his horn and away the thing would go, banging straight into the next one up, to be coupled with the goods train going out on the main line. You'd see the horses and carts coming in from the local warehouses between five and six in the evening, laden with goods to be shipped all over the country. They would unload in Sheffield Street and the goods would be lifted up to the station proper by a hoist.

In those days London Road Station had a big glass dome, similar to Central Station, with a clock over the top. Up the centre of the approach were horse cabs, hansom cabs and the like and at the top was the cabmen's hut and a water trough for the horses. Inside the hut were a stove and chairs and when we played near there they'd call us in and say, "Get sat down, son and eat all these sandwiches and what you can't eat take home." We used to hide in there from the railway police who wanted to throw us off the station!

I was very interested in trains

The approach to London Road Station

and we were always on the station weighing up the different engines. I liked to watch the big expresses going to Euston or, from the other side of the station, the Great Northern trains leaving for Kings Cross. At that time London & North Western was a separate company and there were two lines; the trains to London left practically at the same time and we would watch them going out together. The engines had very short chimneys but were massive, scaling about 150 tons, and were called after titled people: King George V, Prince of Wales and so on. You could see your face in the paintwork and the big, egg-shaped buffers and wheels were silvery and highly polished. The London & North Western's livery wasn't very colourful - just black with red lines on it - but the Midland was a kind of aubergine shade and the Great Central was the most colourful of the lot, with green and gold. Some of the engine drivers would let you on, give you a ride and bring you back again!

A horse operating a turntable at the Great Central warehouse

The Great Central Railway warehouse in Ducie Street

The shops round about were all little corner shops, sometimes in cellars - anywhere they could put on a show. Down the street from us in Chapel Street Billy Grimes sold cigarettes and newspapers. A popular one was the "Illustrated Police Gazette" which was printed on a buff coloured paper and displayed every weekend. Everybody would gather round the shop to look at the gory pictures of murders and the placard would read something like "Man chopped to pieces with an axe teeming with blood". The daily papers, the "Evening News" and "Chronicle" cost a halfpenny each and you could get five Woodbines for the same amount. If you bought a packet of five Players they'd put the matches in free. Copes's cigarettes used to have coupons which you could save up to get an overcoat, a cap, a tie or a shirt. Everybody knew where you'd got it, though - you could always tell a Copes's coat because they were all the same brand. On London Road next to the White Hart you could buy cigarettes by weight: mixed Turkish, Heartsease, Guinea Gold, there were a lot of brands. Where Debenham's (formerly Paulden's) is now was a big cigarette shop called Salmon and Gluckstein's which sold fancy cigarettes of all descriptions.

Everything seemed to be cheap in those days and you could buy small quantities like a pennyworth of sugar or tea, two slices of bread and offcuts of cheese or bacon. Of course, there were no machines then - the cheese was cut by pulling string through it and the bacon was cut with a knife. If you went for a two-pound loaf and it wasn't heavy enough, they cut a chunk off another loaf and threw it on the scales. This was called the "makeweight" and we used to eat it on the way home. Marlands were the great bakers then and my mother, who did her own baking, used to buy all her flour and yeast there.

Milk was brought to the doors by two-wheeled dicky carts and served from a churn. They also came round selling buttermilk, lettuce, crumpets, muffins - one man used to shout "Four-a-penny lemons" and sell them from a bag he had on his back. Others would sell firewood or gas coke from a handcart at a penny a bucket. A fellow who came down our road used to get his from the gas coke yard in Ancoats; his wife was called Annie Cook and we used to shout her name after him. He'd say, "I'll give you a bucket of Annie Cook if you don't get off!" There were a lot of rag-and-bone men too, who would exchange brown stone, cream stone, Yorkshire stone and blue mould for rags.

There was a little chip shop down two steps at the corner of Malaga Street and a clogger's called Manning's on Great Ancoats Street. Mainly we wore clogs with irons toe and heel - a full set of irons cost fourpence and we'd fetch them from the cobblers for our father to put on for us. Sometimes when he didn't want to do it or the old woman was a bit flush she'd say, "Go to Manning's on the Lane and take the clogs with you and get irons on them all." The clogger worked in a cellar and there was a hole in the floor of his shop with two doors you had to lift open to throw the clogs down in a bag. When they were done he opened the doors for you to collect them and one would be at one side of the room and one at the other! That's the way he used to go on.

A row of shops that I used a lot stood on Ancoats Lane nearly opposite Pollard Street. There was a baker's that made their own bread, a tobacconist's, a shop selling soft drinks and sweets, Bill Platt's, the barber's, a Russian Jew who repaired shoes called Morris, a grocer's and a toffee shop on the corner. There were some lodging houses on Chapel Street near the Crown & Sceptre pub and not far away was Jamieson's handcart hire business. Across from the pub, on the corner of Chapel Street and Ancoats Lane, was Nielsen Ladefoged's bacon warehouse, which is still there today. In Bradfield Street alongside the canal Bert Harding had a stable yard and horse-dealing business; there was a horse's head sign over the entrance. Further up that street lived Jack Smith, known as "Pot Jack" because he hawked pots and pans. My mother used to send me to a shop in Goolden's Buildings for bleaching soda when she was washing; they

Old shops on Ancoats Lane in 1985. No.128 (bearing the name S Wilson) was Jack Sibbit's butcher's

sold mottled soap and candles too. The houses round that area were so small they were just like big dog kennels - my mate Charlie Wolstencroft lived in one of them.

Jack Sibbit, the champion cyclist, had a butcher's shop on Ancoats Lane. I can still picture him sitting outside in his striped pinny and straw cady. Not far away was Whitty's herb beer shop; he advertised "Herb Beer and Hop Bitters" made from nettles and herbs and sold in large stone jars with a string top. It was beautiful stuff, great as a livener after a drinking session! There was a good pork butcher's at the bottom of Great Ancoats Street before the First War, run by a German family called Gilbert. They were naturalised and had changed their name to make it sound English, but people still knew their origins and when the war broke out there was a great wave of anti-German feeling. The Gilberts suffered like a lot of foreign families. The shop was wrecked, the windows smashed, black puddings were strewn all over the place and they had to leave - it was in such a state that they couldn't live in it.

The fire station near my school was finished in 1906; it had beautiful flats inside then but they aren't used today. Some of my pals lived there and I would call for them on my way to school. When the bell went the horses would stamp and start about. The harness was fastened in the corner near to the hayrack and the engine and was wired in such a way that when they were called out the collar fell down and they could be harnessed up and away up London Road in minutes. The sparks would fly off the horses' hooves and the fireman would be on the back of the tender

In London Road Fire Station yard in the 1920s

McConnel's mills, from a drawing made about 1905

with the pump, firing up. The bells would be ringing and smoke flying about all over the road. What a sight the first time! I'd never seen anything like it in my life!

Ambulances were also pulled by horses, as were the Black Marias with a policeman on the back, guarding the prisoners in the van. I only went on horse trams a couple of times; people used to walk more then, especially if the weather was bad. Even the motorised, open-top trams were uncomfortable. The seats were hard bench seats and the folk down below would sit huddled up against the rain. If you put an umbrella up on top the wind would blow it inside out. There was no shelter for the driver and when it was snowing all you could see was a white block of snow with the eyes peering out! The number 25 ran down Bradford Road and Bradford Street, past McConnel's mill, on to Great Ancoats Street and down Millers Lane to the terminus at the bottom in Victoria Station. There was a loop line there and it would turn round and come back. The 53 went to Trafford Park and the 59 to Worsley from Thornley Park.

Our Nellie was a doffer at McConnel's and I used to go with her dinner every Monday, Tuesday and Wednesday. The first time I went in on my way to school I was teeming in sweat and frightened to death

Hetherington's works on Chapel Street about 1920

of walking in between the looms. There was only a very narrow space and it was so noisy you couldn't hear them talk. The women were in their bare feet because of the heat and the floors were full of oil. Each one had a big oily patch pinned to her skirt for kneeling down on and these patches were dripping.

All the mills there were supplied by canal and the boats used to tie up near McConnel's where there was a break in the wall with a wooden shutter over it for protection. The boats were bringing coal in all day long and two planks would be run from the boat into the entrance of the mill firehole, which was about five yards away. Men would fill their wheelbarrows with the slack, run along the plank, tip it and back again. They took it as casual work and would get so much an hour.

Opposite McConnel's was a narrow passage where the Brownsfield Mill was and nearby was a pub of the same name. The Brownsfield was the mill where A V Roe made his first aeroplanes, the forerunners

The Brownsfield Mill and McConnel's Mill from the canal in 1985

of the Lancasters and Vulcans. Other firms in the area were Cooper's foundry on Chapel Street and John Hetherington's engineering works. Men went all over the world from there, fitting up machinery. They had a factory on Chapel Street and two on Pollard Street and one of these was later split up and used partly by the Co-op. Shillinglaw & Hulme's at the top of Stony Brow employed mainly women sewing trousers, suits and ladies' wear. Other places where women worked were John Caldwell's and Butterworth's, which dealt in rags. You'd see about five women on a horse and lorry go to the warehouses collecting fents (the clippings). Thompson McKay were agents for the Great Central Railway and Allsopp's had a bottling stores right at the end of the arches on Fairfield Street. Whitbread had no beerhouses in this area then and sold only bottles for the gentry; they too had a bottling place on Store Street and there were two big bonding warehouses on the left of the arch as you were coming away from town. I think these belonged to Bass. On the corner of Boad Street and Store Street was a huge flywheel which drove some hydraulic machinery in the buildings at the rear. I used to watch it in wonder as a boy. It was run by a man called Marshall who also had a shop in Mitchell Street, Beswick.

The streets were full of life then and there was always somewhere to go or something to watch, not least people coming out of the pubs blind drunk at all hours of the day and night! I knew one or two of the "scuttlers" or "Napoo gangs" who were around at the beginning of the First World War. They used to wear red silk ties knotted with the ends flowing and buckled belts, and one gang would fight another but they didn't use weapons, except their belts when they got into trouble. In any case, the coppers soon shifted them.

Life was hard but there was always something to soothe you and people were more together; if anybody was in trouble they'd sit in the house and talk. They went to town properly when they celebrated, too - Christmas was always good. You'd think you were going to have a bad one in our house, then all at once something would come up - the old woman had opened a nest egg somewhere.

Our Arthur was a regular soldier in the 1st Battalion, the King's Own Royal Lancasters, and was one of the first 1914 soldiers to come home on leave from France. He was a sergeant gym instructor, a big fine lad, and he had been in the army eighteen years when he fought at Mons (he was in India for a long time before that). I never came across him when I was in France but he survived the war better than I did - he got a shrapnel wound in his shin bone but it wasn't much and he didn't get a pension for it.

On the canal in the city centre

The people around hadn't seen a soldier from active service until Arthur came home and the neighbourhood was full! The old woman had provided for them - the windows were flung open, there were boxes of beer outside, everybody was welcome. There was a man with a barrel organ who came round to our mother regularly because she would give him a couple of coppers for playing the tune "Faith of our Fathers". He arrived while Arthur was home and Arthur and George Luke, another hefty lad and an ex-sailor, carried the organ off the barrow and into the house. The man said, "I'll have to tell him I've left it here but it'll be all right. It'll only cost you about half a crown." We had it there for a week and there were flags out all over the place!

My first jobs

When I was about eleven years old I found myself working after school for a greengrocer named Jimmy O'Donnell at the bottom of Chapel Street, only about two minutes from where we lived. Later he had a shop on Grey Mare Lane and finished up with one on Ashton New Road. I knew one of his lads and one day when I called round he asked me to sort a box of oranges out and then to go to his stable at Ward's veterinary surgeon's to feed Polly, his pony. I gave the pony a drink, put some corn in the manger, brushed it down and took up its bedding and cleaned it out. When I went back to the shop after half an hour and told Jimmy what I'd done he said, "I didn't tell you to do that, did I?"

"No," I said, "but it's all right, isn't it?"

"Of course it's all right," he said. "You're a handy lad, you are," and asked me to go to the fire station with him after school. I managed to harness the pony myself, we loaded the cart and I was with him until nine o'clock that night, taking orders up and down the steps for the firemen's families. I enjoyed that job and stayed quite a while, calling at the shop every morning before school for my orders. If the alarm went while we were on the fire station landing, the firemen would say, "Don't walk down, slide down the pole," and I would do so with the baskets of fruit and vegetables in my hands!

At the same time as this I worked for a barber named Drinkwater, helping to lather the customers and minding the Drinkwaters' baby, which took to me for some reason. The police headquarters was opposite, so I knew all the policemen who came in for a shave; they used to give me penny and threepence tips. I went on holiday to Southport with this family and occasionally stopped at their house, although my mother didn't like it at first.

A friend and I had another part-time job with a woman named Lucy Tallant at the top of Store Street. She ran a black pudding stall from a table with a cloth on it which she set up at the top of the arch. Our task was to carry the black puddings up to the stall in a pan with a handle on each side. She was well known in the area and people would buy from her at all hours of the day and night. There would be chairs set out, a naphtha lamp on the table and a fire in a bucket if it was winter. She would cut the black puddings up at the stall and salt, pepper and mustard were there if required.

I was only out of work two days after leaving school. In those days, Thompson McKay's, agents for the Great Central Railway, employed lads as "nippers" to watch the carts so that goods weren't stolen and to help the carters collect the paperwork and fill it in. My father wanted to go with me to see about the job but I said, "I can go myself," and went down to the stables to see the man I'd been told to ask for, Jack Harry. Several of my mates, older than me, already worked there and I passed some of them on their way up Stony Brow to the goods yard in Ducie Street.

They told me he was a little fellow and would be arriving

Street entertainment: a barrel organ in Long Millgate, near the Ducie Bridge pub

about 9.00 to 9.15, so when he came I checked up with a workman in the yard that I had got the right man and knocked on his office window. He asked me a few questions and told me to go up to Ardwick Goods Yard on Blind Lane and report to the time office there. He telephoned them to say I was coming and they sent me to ask for a man called Herbert Ackers in the stables. I introduced myself as his helper and that was that!

My starting pay was five bob a week for working from 8.00am to 6.00pm and a shilling rise after twelve months. There were ostlers to look after the horses, which were big shires about sixteen hands high, some of them weighing fourteen to sixteen hundredweight. My carter did very little except drive - I used to load the lorry, check the horse, drop the stuff off at the various stages and get the consignment notes signed. I did most of the work for him. The round was to Hanging Ditch and Withy Grove to the bacon and eggs produce places. Every Tuesday morning we used to take stuff into Strangeways Gaol for the prisoners who were making mail bags: bales of oakum and so on. They'd open one gate to let you through, then lock it behind you before opening the next gate which led into the big yard where the prisoners were.

After about ten months I was told it was better working on passenger services, so I went to see what was available. One of my mates worked on oiling and greasing but that was too dirty a job for my liking, and I was too young for shift work and also for engine cleaning, which I applied for. I was offered a job buffering, oiling the shank so that the buffer would move in and out freely but I didn't fancy it. "We'll give you overalls," they said.
"Yes," I replied, "and you'll need them on that job!"

Eventually I got a job washing out the carriages and checking that they were spick and span down to the handles being cleaned. I also had to fill the diners with water, which I liked doing. On the platform was a tank on two wheels that was full of water and I had to climb up a pair of ladders with the hosepipe, get on to the roof of the train and top up the tanks for the cooking and hot drinks served on the journey.

I did that job for about a year and then I was called into the office for an examination by the station master, Mr Myers. I remember he had a long black beard. They gave me different strands of wool to look at and asked me what colour they were. As a result they decided I was colour blind, so I couldn't go on the footplate as a fireman and progress to engine driver as I would have done otherwise. So I went round looking for employment again.

I found it at Jewsbury & Brown's mineral water factory next to the Territorial Army Barracks at Ardwick Green. The gaffer was called Mr Hayes and he always walked around in a blocker hat. The job was filling soda siphons but there were several lads I knew who worked there and one day we were larking about, squirting the siphons and splashing each other with soda water when the boss walked in! "Out!" he said. "You're sacked." We asked for our wages and "Wages!" he shouted. "You don't deserve any wages. Out! Out!" - and he ran us out of the place.

Games

When we weren't watching the trains at the station or running errands for the grown-ups we used to play all the usual street games. There was "weak horse", where a line of boys used to get down against a wall with one at the helm and the others would leap as far as they

The Territorial Army barracks and Jewsbury & Brown's mineral water works, Ardwick Green

could along their backs. When the load got too heavy for the weakest link, the whole thing collapsed.

We used to make a lot of fun with cigarette cards, though you only got them with the more expensive cigarettes like Gold Flake or Capstan. We would stand one card against the wall and flick another to try to knock it down. If you succeeded, you picked up all the cards which were on the ground. Some lads got great bundles of cards in this way and had really good collections of footballers and so on.

We had a football pitch marked out on Travis Street with coats laid down for goalposts. On Saturday and Sunday afternoons gangs of us played there with a tanner "pill", but there was always somebody dogging out for the copper. If you were caught playing ball games in the street you were fined about ten shillings for causing an obstruction or a nuisance. Johnny Sands, the bookie, sold bits of toys and damaged balls and sometimes he would give us a caseball after the police had chased us off. "Go up the fields and I'll give you a ball to play with," he'd say. Not far away was St Andrew's Square, where the elite lived, and from there a flight of steps led down to Helmet Street Park - we called it "Bunghole Park". There was a shale recreation area where we used to play and they had a bandstand at one time; as young men we had some good times dancing to the bands. The park area is still there but the bandstand has gone.

The Rochdale Canal at the back of the Palace Theatre was always warm, probably because the Dickinson Street Electricity Works pumped their waste into it, and we used to go swimming there straight after school. The police used the bridge on Oxford Street, and they would spot the piles of clothing on the bank and come in from Knott Mill to chase us out of the water. If we were caught we had to go to court and pay a fine but that didn't put us off. Further along was a low wall that was ideal for diving off and the canal there was alive with children swimming in the raw when the weather was warm. We didn't swim in the canals round Ancoats but we did go to the open air bath in Philips Park. It was the coldest water ever invented! People used to joke about that place, "The water's warm now. A man stands at the deep end and pours water from a kettle until you say when!" The nearest Corporation baths were at the back of Mayfield Station; there was a wash-house there as well and we all went there, males and females separately.

In winter you would see kids queuing up at the top of Stony Brow, which was a hill of about one in three with Southern's timber yard at the bottom. We would get ourselves a piece of corrugated tin, bend it at one end, tie a bit of string to it, lie on it and whizz down the footpath right into Southern's gateway. In a bad winter it was just like ski-ing. Oddly enough I

Ancoats Mill Girls' Choir giving a concert in 'Bunghole Park' in 1914

never saw any accidents there until Southern's replaced the brick wall at the bottom with a showroom window displaying different kinds of timber. Then a few went through the windows and eventually they bricked it up again.

There were no outings from school except in the summer holidays, but the Sunday schools ran them and best of all were the ones organised by Wood Street Mission. It didn't matter that we were Catholic - our old woman used to take my brother and I down, we'd get passed by a doctor and they would fix a date for us to go. It cost a shilling for a week at Birkdale Camp, Rotten Row, Southport. On the day we would line up outside the Mission down the side of the John Rylands Library and we would be marched from there down Deansgate to Central Station, boys and girls mixed, though we had different quarters at the camp. There was a bit of jostling on the way but only through excitement at the holiday.

In the games room at Heyrod Street Lads' Club

When we got to the camp the youngsters were in dormitories and those over a certain age in tents, and we all had round pie hats with red bands and blue jerseys with "Birkdale Holiday Camp" written on them in red letters. We played various games - football, shuttlecock and so on - and we were well looked after by the camp leaders who were nice people, both men and women. The only restriction was that you couldn't go out of the camp on your own. There wasn't much emphasis on religion there except that they used to say grace before meals. We handed over our money to the organisers if we had any, and had to apply for it if we wanted it, so as to remove temptation and stop pilfering. Then just before going home we were taken down to the front to buy presents, sticks of rock and so on. For most of us, this was the only chance we had of seeing life outside the city and we really enjoyed the break, though we rarely saw the sea.

I also went on several day picnics from the Wesley Hall, which stood on the corner of Wesley Street and Ancoats Lane. They had a silver prize band at the Hall and held parties for the poor people of the neighbourhood. I went there several times.

Another way of getting out of Manchester was to join one of the boys' clubs: Heyrod Street, Ardwick, Hugh Oldham, Proctor's Gym and others. I belonged to Heyrod Street Lads' Club, which was nearest, and every year we would go away to camp at places like Blackpool

Wood Street Mission children in 1900

and the Isle of Man. We travelled by train and it was a slow journey! You could kick your hat faster than trains could move in those days, or get off in a village, buy some chocolate and get back on again. Heyrod Street was a well established club sponsored by warehouse owners in the town like the O'Hanlon brothers, Barlow & Jones and Captain Helm. Another advantage of being a member was that when you became eligible for work you could go to these firms and if there were any vacancies they would give you a job in one of the warehouses.

There was a lot going on at the club. We had a big basement where you could play football, and there were horizontal bars and rings for gymnastics and spring nets and coconut matting for jumping. All kinds of billiards and other games were played and as well as that we had night school once a week, taken by a man called Chantler. I liked draughts and cards and I played football for one of the teams on a Saturday. The ground was on land owned by Councillor Will Melland and the playing fields are still there today, off Mount Road in Gorton, and are named after him.

The boxing instructor at Heyrod Street was called Pongo Pownall, but if we called him Pongo to his face he used to give us a left hook. There was also a boxing place under the arches next to what was called the cheese arch because it was taken over by a big cheese firm. People who boxed there included the Marchants, Kid Lewis, Louis Ruddick and Kid Furness.

Entertainment

The colliers at Bradford Pit were great fellows for whippet racing and used to go on the fields up Ten Acres Lane. They would throw some kind of ball, slip the dog and time how long it took the dog to catch the quarry. A good slipper would throw a dog about twenty yards - that was the art of the game. You should have seen the food the dogs got, too - new-laid eggs and port wine! They were better fed than the people!

All the colliers had pigeons, if they hadn't got dogs. I was friendly with a little fellow called Jackie Garrity and I used to watch him with his. He would talk about "that blue chequered one" or say, "I'll screw that one's neck; that's no good, that." Johnny Sands had a betting shop on Padgate Street. The shop front was on Adair Street but for betting he used the back because you could go straight into the house from a back entry. When the plain clothes men paid a visit we escaped through the house, into the entry and away!

As I got older and started using the pubs I found out that they all had different characters. They were open from 11.00am to 11.00pm then and most had a piano for entertainment but there'd be other things going on too. I used to work mainly the ones round Stockport Road, Piccadilly and my own area. One very popular one was the Apsley behind the Apollo because it was a good picking-up shop for a bird. A lot of the people from the Ardwick Empire went in there. Behind the station was a big commune and some of the chief pubs in that area were the Shepherd on Chapel Street, "Harry Horner's" (the King Billy on Boad Street) and "Betsy Royle's". The Railway on Chapel Street near Hetherington's works was always called "Abigail's" because it belonged to Abigail Wilkinson. The Minshull on the corner of Rusholme Road was another which did a good trade; Sammy Bland, a corporal in my

Heyrod Street schools, mission hall (centre) and Lads' Club on the right

battalion, married a widow who was the licensee.

I used the pubs in the back streets in town a lot because they never shut. In the Nags Head near the police station you would find yourself rubbing shoulders with policemen after time. Both firemen and policemen used to go in the Prince of Wales in Granby Row, which was on the left hand side past the present Bulls Head.

Angel Meadow was one of the roughest areas in town and there would be all sorts going on in the pubs there. People used to play quoits and darts, there was a lot of ring-throwing and they'd even play throwing corks in a glass to see how many they could get in.

One of our neighbours, Jack Sullivan, who became famous as "Lancashire's Golden Voice", used to sing at the Hen & Chickens on Oldham Street. He lived in St Andrew's Square and was a foreman at Marsden's nut and bolt works in Altrincham Street. (Another famous resident of St Andrew's Square was the jockey, Tod Sloan. He lived in what we called the gentry houses, which had fine spacious lobbies and well laid-out rooms. His sister Edie married a mate of mine and lived in Dearden Street; their daughter, Dolly Prestbury, lives in Belle Vue today.) The Hen & Chickens had all sorts of customers. Foy, one of the landlords, had a daughter who married the heavyweight boxer, Boy McCormick; they later kept the Crown & Kettle. He was a picture of a fellow, six-foot three-inches tall with a fine head of red hair and about fifteen-and-a-half stone. He was an orphan, brought up in St Joseph's Home, Longsight, fought with Dempsey's stable in America in the thirties and did really well. Then when he came back here he got mixed up with some of the bad characters in Oxford Street and went downhill. When his wife met him he was canvassing tea, carrying a case about and knocking on doors.

When we lived in Every Street we were right opposite the "Blind Man's" (the Star Inn) on the corner of Russell Street. Ernie Vaughan was the licensee there and Albert McKenna had a greengrocer's on the other corner. The Hallams ran the Mitchell at the corner of Holt Town. Billy McLeod, the boxer, used to preach outside the Star and the Mitchell with a naphtha lamp over his head when it got

The Apsley Cottage - a good picking-up shop!

A view of Granby Row and the Prince of Wales in 1920

dark. He had been a prize fighter, then reformed and joined the Salvation Army, who set him up in a pot shop on Beswick Street. The Salvation Army band used to go in procession down Ashton New Road and along Every Street and Junction Street - after closing time all the drunks would fall in behind them and follow them into the hall to sleep it off.

The Peveril of the Peak down by the Hippodrome used to be a good pub. The theatre was where the Gaumont is now and at the interval the theatricals used to slip out of the stage door with all their powder and paint on right into the Pev. Men used to come round the pubs doing illusions like pulling rabbits out of hats while you were sitting at the table - a lot harder than being on a stage. Ventriloquists would come in too and they'd have a whip round after they had done their act - anything to get a copper.

There were a lot of theatres in Manchester in those days and I used to go two or three times a week, mainly to the Ardwick Empire, the Hippodrome and the Palace and occasionally to the Metropole. I never went to Queens Park Hipp or anywhere like that, nor to the big shows - I was more interested in variety. I saw Gertie Gitana, George Lashwood, Talbot O'Farrell, Kate Carney, George Robey and Formby, the father of the famous one. My favourite was Jose Collins and I remember seeing her at the Princes', which was a musical theatre on Oxford Street. Tuesday nights were the best, when all the mill girls used to go with their clogs and shawls on; it was twopence in the gallery with seats like wooden stairs and you'd have clogs in your back. As we grew up we started going in the posh seats!

Peter Street had several theatres and music halls including the Theatre Royal, the Midland Hotel Theatre and variety theatres like the Tivoli and the Grand. The Grand was near the lights on the junction with Deansgate. It's a car salesroom now but if you look at the side you'll see some square windows above the shop which remain from the old theatre. The Tivoli was on the opposite side of the road near Watson Street.

A gang of us used to go to watch silent movies every Friday night at a place called the Secular Hall on Rusholme Road; you came out on Oxford Road near the Grosvenor. It was an old mission hall which they'd turned into a picture house and an old woman there used to play the piano accompaniment to the films by candlelight. Later I saw the first talking movie, "The Jazz Singer".

There was a picture house called the Cosy Corner on Swan Street in the twenties, not far from the clothes market where the plant hawkers swapped plants for clothes which they later flogged at the auctions. After all the pubs had shut in the afternoon the Cosy was full of people sleeping off the morning session. The toilets were situated near the screen and the patrons would shout, "Get out of the ****ing road!" to the unfortunate boozers who had to go. The building was taken over later by Smalley's, the paper merchant's.

Finally there was the Coliseum, next to the Ardwick Hippodrome, where I met my Waterloo!

Joining up

One Saturday in February 1915 some of my mates said, "Let's go the the Col. There's a recruiting meeting on," so we went down to Ardwick Green to watch. After the show there was a "go as you please" competition with people playing mouth organs, spoons, "rickers" (bones) and then came the appeal for volunteers for the army: "Come up on stage!" One by one men mounted the steps to the recruiting officer and my mate asked me, "Are you coming up?"

The Palace on Oxford Street in the 1890s

"I don't know," I said. "Are you?"

Then Tommy Clements decided he would go. It was all right for him - he was old enough at nineteen to sign on but I had just left sixteen years of age. He told me to think of a date in 1915, knock off nineteen years and give that as my birth date. In the end four of us went up, including my best pal, Tommy Bunner, and when we got on stage the band was playing and the audience were shouting "Hurrah!" and singing patriotic songs.

We were marched across the road to where the Apollo car park is now. Then it was the private gardens of a doctor's house and we lined up on his lawns waiting to be examined. I passed my medical there at one o'clock on the Sunday morning - as long as you were breathing you were in! Then we were marched to the barracks, given a shilling and told to report to Ardwick Green Barracks at 9.00am the next day. That was how I came to be in the Eighth Battalion, Manchester Regiment.

On the Monday we were given our army numbers and kitted out. Tommy's number was 4857 and mine was 4858, though it was changed later to 301678. Wilf Taylor, the quartermaster sergeant, issued us with overcoat, pullover, knife, fork and spoon, razor, lather brush and kitbag and then we were sent home for the time being. It was the practice for new recruits to sleep at home until there were sufficient men to form a company and most didn't put the uniform on unless they were going to the barracks. You were given rational allowance to keep you while you stayed at home!

However, in my case I wasn't there long enough to claim it. When I broke the news to my mother that I had joined up she said, "I'll be at that barracks in the morning!" For some reason she didn't get there on the Monday and on the Tuesday we were on our way to the train to Southport. The day before we had been marched round the town centre to drum up support - they must have liked the look of us!

My billet in Southport was next to the Post Office at 31 Gordon Avenue with a very nice lady, Mrs Grice. Eight soldiers were billeted with her and we had some good fun while we were there. Each morning roll call took place in the road in front of the house and being lined up outside on a cold winter's morning didn't appeal to me, so I found a way round it. I would lift up the window, listen for my name to be called, shout, "Here, sergeant," then bang down the window and go back to bed. Then one morning the sergeant tipped to what I was doing. "I'll give you, 'Here, sergeant'!" he said.

We did our training at a place called Crossens just outside Southport and it was pretty severe; most of our instructors were regular army men. They would have us running along the sands first thing in the morning, shirt necks open, braces dangling and canvas slippers on. When we went back to our lodgings the old woman had the table set with taters and bacon for breakfast and we all dived in. We were sixteen to nineteen years old and as fit as fighting cocks! By this time we had been equipped with full khaki uniforms and issued with long Lee Enfield rifles and we would march along the promenade every morning with the band playing. We used to see an old salt there, about six feet tall

April 1915: A Field Kitchen in Albert Square, part of the recruitment drive for the Manchester Regiment Service Battalions

with a weatherbeaten face and flowing white beard, dressed in a blue jersey and black pants. He looked just like Sifta Sam in the salt adverts! As we passed him he would say, "There's VCs among you," and after this had happened several times we all sang out, "There's VCs among us!" every time we marched by.

From Southport we went to Codford on Salisbury Plain. What a tester of a place that was! It was the winter of 1915, we were up to our knees in mud and slutch and you could hear the rats gnawing away at the wood of the army huts we slept in. There were rats all over the place - some of them bald-headed ones fourteen hands high!

After about two months of that we were moved to a place called Witley in Surrey which was much better country. In the middle of the hut was a big combustion stove and the bedding consisted of three trestles, three boards and a palliasse that had to be filled with straw every week. They delivered the straw in large bales which had to be unloaded and stored in a dry place, which was easier to find at Witley than at Codford.

I had barely five months' training but that was my own fault because I volunteered for a draft. The old soldiers had told me about this bull business and said I wouldn't have to do it if I went on foreign service. "You'll find a difference in life abroad," they said. "Polishing here, polishing there - there's none of that abroad." They were right!

I sailed on the Arcadian one Sunday night from Devonport and it was a marvellous sight to see the long queue of men patiently waiting to board. We sailed out in pitch darkness, a marine at each end of the ship manning a machine gun and a destroyer escorting us part of the way.

The Middle East

It took us sixteen days to reach Alexandria and we had a very rough passage through the Gulf of Lions, just off Marseilles, It's a good job all the plates were enamel - they were sliding all over the floor! No-one was allowed on the top deck unless they were on guard duty and several people were injured. It seemed as though the propeller was missing the water and threshing the air; the boat would lift up with a "Bung! Bung!" noise and then drop down again suddenly. We all had to do a spell on the top deck watching out for submarines and from there you could see the three destroyers. One minute they were there, the next they had vanished as if into thin air, then they reappeared moments later. I thought we were never going to reach Alexandria. We did make one stop at Malta for recoaling but we weren't allowed ashore.

We had only just arrived in Egypt when we learned that we were to go to the Dardanelles and we moved off, stopping at Mudros harbour on the isle of Lemnos on the way. Mudros was the chief port for the operations in Gallipoli. I was lucky because we finally reached the peninsula in the winter of 1915, shortly before the campaign ended and I never got to the front. We were in support on W Beach with the Aussies to the left of us and the 11th Division to our right. The 29th Division was in the first landings. The evacuation was the finest piece of work they did on Gallipoli. We were told not to get panicky and work to the orders they gave us and storage and troops were moved out in forty-eight hours without a single casualty. It was a masterpiece!

Saying goodbye. Men of the Manchester Regiment Service Battalions at London Road Station, en route for Grantham in April 1915

We went back through the Suez Canal, leaving some troops at Port Said, disembarked at Port Suez and marched from there to a camp in the middle of the desert called El Kantara. In time the railway was extended and El Kantara became the base camp where everything was assembled for our attack on the Turks. When enough troops and supplies had arrived we were told to establish redoubts but it was impossible to dig trenches because of the sand, so we were given latticing and sandbags and had to build up defences from that.

Then we went north to El Ferdan and prepared to make an attack. We were stationed there for quite a long time and from the base we made regular patrols out into the desert. The area in front of the battalion was patrolled by cavalry - the Australian Light Horse went out every night scouring the countryside. It *was* countryside! Just wild desert with no roads and not a thing in sight. Reveille was at 3.00am before sunrise so that our work could be finished before it got too hot and during the day the temperature went up to between 115° and 120° in the shade. The sand was too hot to walk on then - it would burn the flesh.

We met people on that desert who were never seen before! There were Bedouin tribesmen with their women and children on camels, and cocks, hens, goats and all their animals trailing along behind. How they lived I'll never know, because there was nothing growing there. Still, they never bothered with us at all and we didn't trouble them. It was all camel work in the desert - horses were no use. The Egyptian Labour Corps were with us, transporting water, rations and supplies and you could see the camel caravans stretching right back across the desert. Some of the Australians were villains with them - I've seen a steel whip used on an Egyptian camel boy. There was no heavy artillery, just mounted guns and the camels carried those too.

We first came into contact with the Turks at a place called Hill 40, but we soon disposed of them. Getting there was worse than the battle itself! You couldn't travel very fast in the desert conditions and we had to attach wire netting to our boots to make them a bit like snowshoes so that we wouldn't sink in the sand. We marched at least ninety miles in four days. That was a test! We had very little water - about one bottleful each, I think - and we weren't allowed to go near any of the wells in case they were poisoned. Officers stopped us from approaching them. You can imagine what that was like! Men were falling out like rotten sheep and out of about fifty in my platoon only a handful of us finished.

Our platoon officer was Lieutenant Jackson from S & J Watts and quite a few of our officers were connected with leading Manchester firms. The adjutant was Jock Horsfall from one of the large taxi cab businesses and there was Captain Barlow of Barlow & Jones', Captain Frankenburg of the Greengate works in Salford, Colonel Moore and an O'Hanlon of the warehousing firm in Dale Street.

Our next skirmish was at Katia but they didn't put up much of a fight. The Aussie cavalry's night patrols put us wise to the Turkish formations and after a few clashes they retreated to El

A British column on the march in the desert

Arish. It was all done in the boiling sun and there was no shade anywhere. Men kept dropping from exhaustion and sickness and there were bodies lying in the path of our advance. Stretcher bearers were doing their best to cope with the worst cases, but a camel ride is a terrible experience for a man who is sick or in pain. When they start off one stretcher's on the ground and the other's in the air and after a few steps they are going up and down like yo-yos! The camel's gait across the sand is very jerky and the hump on its back makes it difficult to load things evenly. El Arish was the final point for our battalion and we turned back from there - we had to, there were no men left! By that time corporals were in charge of a company - shocking!

Our final stop in Egypt was at Moascar near Ismailia, for a rest. It was a lovely place, called "the garden city of Egypt", with separate Arab and French quarters. We spent about three weeks there, recuperating and getting the battalion fit. Apart from fatigues parties and guard duties we had brass band concerts, football and various games. Those were my happiest memories of Egypt, but the fun didn't last very long. We soon sailed from Ismailia to Marseilles en route for the Western Front.

France

We arrived in France in March 1917 and went straight up the line to a village called Peizieres, near Epehy, where they came out of the line for a rest in the back. Most of the places we passed had been well and truly battered, it was the worst winter for many years and we were quartered in an old, broken-down barn with hardly any slates. A tarpaulin was spread across the roof but it made little difference. We were frozen to the marrow. Everybody was fed up, coming to that after the boiling heat of the desert. It's a wonder we had any troops left at all!

I'll never forget the first night in the front line at Epehy. The moon was just rising and it was very quiet, though we could hear the sound of artillery in the distance and see the flashes where fighting was taking place. Brigadier-General Ormsby, who was in charge of the 127th Brigade, came past on his charger. A few weeks later he was killed by a piece of shell at Catelet Copse. In daylight we could see for miles but we never saw any sign of the Germans - no trench works or anything. They were obviously waiting for something to happen but we moved away from there after about three weeks.

Our rations were atrocious - we rarely had any bread and instead we were given large biscuits, hard as rocks, like the ones they feed to dogs nowadays. The bully beef in tins was very nice but you got fed up with it day in, day out. Maconochies (a stew) made a fine meal - if you were given one of those you thought you were in heaven, but you didn't get them very often. Usually one tin was shared between three men but now and again you would get a full one. When we were in the reserve lines my mate and I used to mooch around the little country towns looking for a bakehouse, but the bakers were scared to death of the military police and refused to let us buy any bread, despite our trying day after day. In action we just ate when we could, when things were quiet. We carried an iron ration with us at all times which we were supposed to eat only if we were cut off and if we were given permission. Many times we had to throw them away because they were green mouldy!

When we left Epehy we passed through a place called Havrincourt, which was beautifully quiet chalk country.

Lancashire Territorials digging trenches in the desert

We made it a hell hole. First our artillery opened up sending barrages over, then the Germans replied. They were the "Anglo-Saxon Germans" who were supposed to be friendly - if you didn't fire, they wouldn't bother. We went out one night taking picks, shovels, rolls of barbed wire and stakes and advanced the line 750 yards. We put the barbed wire out and began digging trenches but it started raining when we got two feet down and we had to go back and try again the next night. We finished the line and sandbagged it and then the Germans didn't half give it a hammering! We lost a few then.

About this time my platoon corporal, Fred Glover, was puffing away at his pipe on the fire step one night and I was on sentry duty. Suddenly I saw blood on him and told him about it. "What are you talking about?" he said.
"It's you! You've been hit in the arm!" We got a stretcher bearer and the next time I saw him he was outside Creamer's lodging house on Grosvenor Street after the war, a red-haired fellow with his arm off. I said hello and asked how long he had been like that. "Since that night you told me there was blood running down my arm - it was gashed right through to the other side and they had to take it off," he said. "I live here now."

Bullecourt was another hell hole which changed hands week in and week out. Nobody could hold it because it had been battered so much by the artillery of both sides. There wasn't a square inch of ground that wasn't ripped up by shell fire. It had been a village of small houses with us dug in on one side and the Jerries on the other, so close that there was a lot of hand-to-hand fighting. By the time I got there the houses had been shelled so we stayed on the outskirts.

When we got near Arras I was in a working party attached to the Royal Engineers. The job was to dig tunnels under the German lines, plant explosives and then blow them up. We had some lovely underground quarters there with a light railway, electric lights and beds to sleep in when we finished our shift. There were locked doors at intervals along the passage and one night one of the miners with us said, "Come and listen to him working." You could hear the Germans digging on the other side!

Twenty of us went out on patrol from there one night to get a sniping post that had been causing us some trouble and we brought some prisoners in for interrogation. One of them, who was wearing the uniform of the Hanover and Wurttemberg Fusiliers, had been a chef at the Grand Hotel in Manchester and spoke perfect English. When I asked him how he came to be fighting he said, "I was on my bleeding holidays when I came here and it stuck to me! I couldn't get away!" Sometimes you got to know the reputation of the units facing you. Another lot of prisoners we brought in said, "We've heard about you, the 42nd Division from Egypt."

We marched an average of 24km a day in France with a full fifty-pound pack consisting of blankets, groundsheet, plimsolls, underwear, overcoat and other kit, entrenching tool, 120 rounds of ammunition (5x24 clips) and a rifle. Later, when I was put on a Lewis gun, I was glad to get rid of that lot. There were six of us in a team and I was number one, so apart from my pack I only had the gun, a revolver and a pouch of bullets. Someone else carried the ammunition for the Lewis gun. The only thing they looked after was our feet - after each day's march the puttees and two pairs of socks would come off and the stretcher bearers would treat our feet with whale oil and camphor powder. The rest of our clothes had to stay on!

An artist's impression of the fighting at Bullecourt

Very occasionally we would ride on French trains, which had wooden seats and did about four miles per hour. If you came to a level crossing you could go and do an hour's shopping before the train started again! Sometimes people who had nipped off for some smokes could be seen running up the track after the train, and they nearly always caught it.

At one point we got a young officer from the Buffs; a Londoner. He was a real bastard. It's a good job he didn't stay long as someone had promised that if we went over he wouldn't be certain of coming back. We had a great bunch of lads in the battalion, most of them from the Manchester area, but with a draft from the South Lancashires. We had a good set of sergeants, too, Sergeants Whalley, Nolan and Lear and a good corporal. Sergeant Lear got shot by a South Lancs lad from Liverpool! They had fallen out at the side of the road for a ten minute rest and the habit was to squat down with your rifle between your legs and the safety catch on. The Scouser was next to me and Sergeant Lear was standing in front of him. All at once there was a bang and the sergeant got shot right through the shoulder. The lad must have forgotten to put his safety catch on and caught the trigger with his finger.

This same fellow was a real nuisance when we were fighting. Every time we went into the line he wanted to give himself up, but he wanted someone to go with him! He would say to me, "Do you fancy giving yourself up? I'll go if you'll go," and I would reply, "Go on your own. You keep talking about it but you don't do it." He'd go on, "You won't get away from here alive," and in the end I said, "I wish you'd **** off! Get up to the other end of the line!" I don't know what happened to him because I never saw him again after I was wounded.

The only time I fought with the French was at a place between Arras and Lens. The short ladders were there where they had been going over the top and there were still dead lying in the trenches. I don't know how long they had been there but they had had a real hammering.

From there I got sent to Nieuport on the banks of the Yser Canal and we had to patrol in boats because the land had been flooded by the Belgians. There were duckboards in the underground passages and when the water rose at night they floated. The headquarters there was called Indiarubber House because the bombs used to ricochet off it, but the Germans kept shelling it. I was amazed by the big naval guns at Nieuport. They were mounted on railway lines and after they had fired the truck rushed back into the concrete tunnel and the doors would shut. After an interval the gun would fire again. Every night a caterpillar vehicle came up, pulling a truck with about twelve shells on it. They were about five feet long, the width of the truck, yet when the gun was fired all there was was a puff of smoke and a dull thud.

At that time they were firing on Roulers, near Passchendaele, about twelve miles away. The crew were from the Naval Division - that is, sailors and marines who weren't needed at sea and had been transferred to fight on land. They were under naval discipline but were dressed like soldiers.

In the autumn of 1917 I was allowed home for seven days' leave. I put new clothes on, but when I arrived my mother made me take them off and put them in the back yard because they were ridden with lice. Most of

At the Yser Canal

us had lice by then - we hadn't taken our uniforms off for months - and they are very difficult to get rid of once you pick them up.

On leave at the same time was a lad called Tom Taylor, who was nicknamed the Mad Slater because when he got drunk he used to climb ladders and run about the rooftops and guttering. We couldn't get a drink anywhere - the pubs had no beer. Then Tom told me about some barrels which were scotched-up outside the Manchester Brewery Company waiting to be loaded on to the drays. This was only about five or six minutes' walk from our house and the route was all downhill, so we knocked some of the scotches away and rolled a barrel down Chapelfield Lane, where Moseley's Rubber Works was, under the arch of Fairfield Street and down St Andrews Street into our street. We set it up on bricks, Tom shouted, "Fetch out your buckets and your jugs!" and all the neighbours were drunk as lords all day! The day after a car rolled up and the gentleman commented, "You seem to be enjoying yourselves." We offered him a drink but he said, "I'm from the brewery and we're looking for this." We explained that we had to go back to France after seven days and he said we could have the drink but asked us to bring the barrel back - apparently it was worth more than the beer! When we did this, the brewery people thanked us, offered us a drink of what we wanted, wished us luck and gave us some cigars.

Shortly after I returned from leave we were fighting in the Ypres salient around Poperinge, Vlamertinge, Ypres itself and the Menin Road. That and the Sinai Desert were the two worst areas I saw. The desert was a test of endurance and Ypres a test of slaughter. We were lousy, hungry and surrounded by pools of water stinking with the dead bodies in them. All the rations, stocks and ammunition had to pass that way to get to that part of the sector so the Germans used to have firing periods at night and if you got through you were lucky. Ypres itself had once had a Cloth Hall which was just like Albert Square's double but when I got there hardly anything stood and there were heaps of bricks everywhere.

The station was badly knocked about and we were underneath the prison in a corrugated "elephant hut" with debris on top of it. Towards the line there was hardly a level piece of road anywhere; the gun pits were in shell holes and the guns were wheel to wheel.

Nearly all the transport was done by the ASC (later the RASC) using mules. Like donkeys they didn't need much food and they didn't need shoes, though every so often you had to pare and clean their feet. The mules I had seen in the city were mostly small in size but some of the army ones were fifteen hands high. They were good grafters, but talk about stubborn! If they dug their heels in that was that until they changed their minds.

From Ypres we went to Armentieres, which was another warm shop. Here and elsewhere we used heavy tanks which could go over walls and we did a lot of advancing behind them. You could hear them coming from miles away. But the next major campaign I took part in was at La Bassee. The Portuguese were with us there and you've never seen such a ragged-arsed army in your life! They wore a grey-green uniform

The ruins of the Cloth Hall, Ypres, in the last days of the war

and quite a few of them got shot in mistake for Jerries. When there was a bombardment they needed a regiment behind them to keep them there, otherwise they used to run off all over the place. The front roughly followed the line of the canal and we went in and out of Festubert, Givenchy and La Bassee itself, fighting the Prussian Guards. A lot of our Guards were there too - I saw Coldstreams, Grenadiers and Irish Guards - and a lot are buried there. It was an uncomfortable place to be: the area was full of brickfields and sugar factories and when there was a bombardment there was a lot of red dust in the front line, enough to choke you. We did two hours on duty and four off and during the four off we could sleep in candlelit tunnels, but we kept our packs on. Once when I woke up I heard a scuffle - it was rats in my back pack after my iron rations!

We saw a fair range of weapons at La Bassee: "flying pigs", shells with propellers on the back and "minis", fired by the Germans from small cannon. There were things called "Jack Johnsons" which didn't half make big holes - you could get a warehouse in one. You could see these coming towards you if you were on the receiving end but the whizz-bangs were the worst. They were only used over short distances but the velocity was terrific - the shell would burst before you heard the gun fire. I also saw the liquid flame the Germans used here - the weapon shot a long petrol flame from a cylinder, like an early kind of flame-thrower - and La Bassee was the only place where I saw phosgene gas ready for use. It came in big cylinders which would be put on the back of the trench with pipes running from them. We didn't use it much because it was too easy to gas yourself if the wind changed. It's a very heavy gas and travels slowly about eighteen inches off the ground, but it will drop into any hollows and stay there for days or weeks. It looks like white steam and you can see it coming a mile away so you've got all the time in the world to put your gas mask on, but it's one of the worst gases. To test ourselves we used to go into a live chamber with a gas mask on and lift the mask up for a couple of seconds. You should have seen the state of our clothing when we came out - it goes green, buttons, uniform and all.

The reserve lines were near a place called Bethune and one night my mate and I discovered a camp of the Chinese Labour Corps a short distance away. They did all the rough jobs on the roads like repairing and rebuilding. In those days I would do anything to make a bob or two, so we took a jack-knife, a cut-throat razor and several other things and went into this camp to see what we could get for them. We peeped into a hut where they were all seated around a big stove in the corner and one of them signed to us that they had food. He put his hand in my pocket, searching for my swag, then led us down to a table where there was a stack of bowls piled high with rice and gave us some chopsticks. We couldn't make them understand that we wanted bread and when we did eventually get through to them they didn't have any. While we

The Menin Road

were in the hut German bombers came and buzzed the area so they put the lights out and dropped down on the floor. In the scramble that followed they finished up in a corner piled on top of each other! I said to my mate, "They know the sound of Jerry's planes, all right." Then he started bombing so we made our way back to the reserve lines. If we had been caught, we'd have got twelve months in jail!

We saw a lot of German planes flying along the trench-lines machine-gunning us. You could see the pilots laughing at you as you dropped flat on to the trench floor. Our planes did the same to the Jerries and these attacks caused a lot of casualties on both sides. It was interesting to watch the dog-fights that took place high above the trenches, each pilot trying to out-manoeuvre his opponent so that he could shoot him down. They were in open cockpits with no cover from the elements - it was rough in those days in the Royal Flying Corps! I think the average speed was about 115mph and the most common planes were Sopwith Camels, Avros and Handley Pages. I used to like watching them observing for the Royal Artillery. When an objective came into view they relayed where the shells were dropping and how far off-target they were, using a signal lamp to flash back the hits in Morse Code. They were clever at it. In fact I've been behind an RA battery when they received the messages from the plane and seen them resetting their sights and the plane registering their hits. If anything went wrong the pilots had to try to land the aircraft, or jump out if the plane caught fire and they were still alive. In this respect the pilots of the observation balloons were luckier - they had parachutes! If Jerry shot them down, as he did one after another, they could bail out and stand some chance of landing alive.

Shortly before the big German attack in March 1918 we were having lessons on the blackboard and I was given charge of a Lewis gun. They knew right to the day when the attack would be and we were sent southwards from La Bassee and told to be on the alert. If we hadn't been ready the Germans would have gone right through to the sea, but we were ready! As it was we started way past Havrincourt and he chased us so far back down the line that at night time we were passing through the town of Havrincourt itself. We bypassed Vimy Ridge near Thiepval about this time and I could see for miles across fields flat as a billiard table. The masses of German infantry showed up as one block of field grey coming right across country, our shells dropping amongst them as they advanced towards our lines. If we had made a stand then the war might have ended differently because Jerry had fresh men rushed from the Eastern front after the Russian ceasefire. But we let him advance and advance and finally his lines were stretched too far and we were able to hold him and start pinching back bits of land here and there.

There was a bit of a lull for a few months after this and we had some fun during periods of rest in the reserve lines behind Havrincourt. Our own Divisional concert party, the 42nd Bluebirds, contained two Queens Park men who used to tread the boards in Manchester, Danny Miller and a lad called Shufflebottom. Percy Lawler from Ashton was a good step dancer and there was a funny

Men of the 1/4th East Lancashire Regiment with the 42nd Division near Givenchy

Irish comedian, McGinty. We had good football and boxing teams and competed against other Divisions. We held our own against the 1st Scottish Horse, many of whom played for teams like Rangers, with our own local lads from Ardwick Green. Colonel Moore was our goalie; he was a fine fellow, six-foot-three-inches tall. There was a lovely boxing arena at Marieux where an ammunition dump had been blown up. The bottom of the crater was a clay cone and they had put seats round this with the boxing ring at the bottom.

In the summer of 1918 I found myself in a place called Trescault, where there were a lot of Australian troops. A mate of mine and I were a bit in credit so we clubbed together to start a crown-and-anchor board. The Aussies loved it and we were having a burster - we lived like lords for a short time. People were asking for our rations because we could afford to dine in the local estaminets! Shortly afterwards when I was wounded I had 750 francs on me as well as a Walther revolver, a real beauty, that I had taken from a German officer. When I woke up after the operation there wasn't a penny left! All there was in my pocket was my pay book and a bundle of field cards stuck together with blood. I had heard of this happening to other people; the RAMC were nicknamed "Rob All My Comrades" by some of the troops. If there was anything of value on you when you went in, you could bet ten shillings you wouldn't find it when you woke up.

The British counter-attack proper began in August 1918. By then the German offensive had run out of steam and our attack finished him off. We cleared trenches where they had been dug in for some time and took many prisoners as well as their rifles, ammunition and rations. Casualties were high and we were sent to relieve the Naval Division. We took over from them in a sunken road near Le Barque and one lad told me they had lost hundreds in their advance. All round were scattered pieces of khaki clothing with flesh and bones inside where the men had been blown to fragments. It was here that I was badly wounded and here that I saw two of my mates shoot themselves with captured German rifles to get out of it.

On the Western Front: men of the Manchester Regiment resting in the shelter of a disabled tank

We had had some success and as I left the trench a big shell came over and burst about twenty-five yards in front of me, making a big crater. I said, "Let's make for that. He'll not put another there." I placed the Lewis gun on top and everybody got nicely settled in, but the next shell he sent over didn't burst on the ground, it burst in the air and dropped all the shrapnel on top of us! It took my left hand off and came down through my steel helmet, scarring my face. I picked myself up and ran back to the trench leaving behind my gun and equipment. My hand was held by a piece of flesh and it banged and slapped as I ran. Blood was pumping all down my face and on to my uniform. By the time I had scrambled into the trench and sat on the fire step I couldn't move an eyelid. I was prostrate! The stretcher bearer shouted for another to help him and they left the stretcher on top and jumped down beside me. He began to bandage my hand and I said, "Cut it off - there's nothing there. It's no use like that," but he said, "No, no, I'll patch it up all right," and he made a good job of it, cutting my sleeve with a pair of scissors. Between them they made me comfortable on the stretcher in the bottom of the trench and put my arm in a splint. Then one of them asked, "Can you keep a secret, Mick? We're going to do ourselves in." "Are you?" I said. "Well, move me further down the trench, then, away from where you are!"

After they had moved me I was facing them and saw all that happened. They couldn't use British weapons because they would have been found out and charged with SIW (Self-Inflicted Wounds), so they got a German rifle, put a bullet in the breech and the first one had his in the leg just above the ankle. The blood shot out as from a hosepipe for a second or two, then it stopped. He whipped his puttee off and placed a bandage round it, put another round in the breech and said, "Right, mate, where do you want yours?"

"I'll have mine in the arm," was the reply.

"Keep your arm still, then," and he duly obliged! They told me it was the only way out. "Nobody will get away from here alive. It's terrible outside - there's plenty of dead on top," and he knew because he had been on top.

I knew that this was the end of army days for me. Shortly afterwards Captain Forbes came in and looked at me and asked how I was. I said, "Rough!" and he promised, "We'll soon have you away," and shouted for Bill Hibbert, saying that they would get me moved down the line as soon as possible.

The first place I went to was a bell tent, where I had my first operation. My arm was going septic and they removed part of my wrist. I remember a man dabbing at my head with the anaesthetic all the time I was there, and every time I came round he gave me a drop more. I never felt a thing! I could hear the shells whistling over and the clay falling on the tent, so I knew Jerry wasn't far away! Then I remember being driven in an RAMC motor ambulance to the field dressing station, a school in a nearby village. There were four of us in the back and we were tossing and turning the whole way because of the shell holes. A friend of mine, Jack Welsby, was there when I was admitted. Years later at Ardwick Barracks he told me that they had had me in the operating room for two and three-quarter hours. From there I was transferred to the 1st Australian General Hospital at Etaples, near Boulogne. I was there a week and then came home to Blighty.

When we arrived at Southampton we were unloaded from the hospital ship and put on to the railway platform with large luggage labels round our necks, ready for loading on to the hospital train: we were due to go to Leith Naval Hospital. An ambulance man offered me a cigarette. My face was heavily bandaged but I could still smoke, so I thanked him and asked him where the hospital train on the opposite platform was going. "That's going to Manchester," he said. "It should arrive in Mayfield about ten o'clock tonight." I asked him and his mate to carry me over and I was only there about ten minutes before they started loading the train. I was first on, we were in Manchester by 8.30pm and I was taken to C Division police headquarters. This was 5th September 1918 and I finished up in Grange Street, only a cock stride from where we lived. That's how I worked my loaf to get home. I had managed to fling a letter for my mother into the crowd which met the train, someone passed it on to her and next morning all my friends were at the hospital to see how I was going on.

Grange Street had been a school originally - it was common in those days to convert a school into a hospital. When I'd been there about a month I was up on my feet and walking about all right and the sister asked me, "How would you like to go to the theatre? I've got some

A British transport column moving back through a Somme village in March 1918

tickets for the Metropole at Openshaw." I was glad to go and during the interval I felt a tap on my shoulder. Who should it be but my mate who had shot himself in the leg when I was wounded! "Bloody hell!" I said. "Where are you?"

"I'm at Alma Park School, Levenshulme." He was walking with a stick then. The other mate who was wounded in the arm lived in Liverpool and they hadn't met since returning to England but this one lived in Levenshulme. Later he got a job driving for the CWS in Balloon Street but I haven't seen him for years.

I remember Armistice Day for a different reason. There was a fellow in our battalion who used to volunteer for night patrols, but he would kill the enemy before he would take prisoners and in the end nobody would go with him. He finished up being decorated but he was a wild lad and they had to get him out of the guardroom to give him his Military Medal! I went down to watch the Armistice celebrations - I remember I was still in the blue uniform they gave the wounded in hospital - and who should I see but this fellow being held down by four policemen. He had kicked in the window of the tailor's at the corner of Newton Street!

The 1914 men were treated very badly after the war. They bluffed us with that saying, "A land fit for heroes to live in." I used to go twice a year to be photographed sideways, frontwards and backwards to see if there was any improvement, so they could drop my pension. They used to put a tape measure on you! Before it was made permanent I had to go down to Bury Old Road once a year for examination and the last doctor I saw said, "Who's sent you here?"

"The Ministry of Pensions," I said.

He said, "Put your hat on and go home. It's a bloody disgrace to send men with limbs off. There's nothing we can do for them."

You had to have a limb off to keep your pension - if you had any wounds, you were finished! If two limbs were missing you got 33/- per week (later £2) and it went down from there. There were fellows there who were bloody broken-hearted.

To get anything like justice you had to play the system. When I was first examined a doctor said to me, "I suppose you know you've still got metal left

Emily Robinson and Margaret Atherton. Maggie was a girlfriend before Mick joined the army and both girls went to see him in hospital when he came back from France. The photo was taken when the girls were crane drivers at Armstrong - Whitworth's in Openshaw

in your head?" I didn't, but I pretended to and said it was giving me a lot of trouble. I've played on that ever since, telling them I'd got head pains and a discharge from the ears. Years later one Scots doctor said, "Have you had a holiday? I suppose you can't afford it. Would you like to go away for a few weeks?"

I said, "I'll go anywhere!" He sent me to Mosley Hill in Liverpool for seven weeks and I got in with some lads from Liverpool who showed me round.

Those of us who came back from the war ended up at the Labour Exchange - mine was at Whitworth Hall on Oxford Road. I got 29/- a week for three months, then £1 and after six months it was dropped to

Limbless ex-servicemen at Queen Mary's Hospital, Roehampton, in 1919. Mick is on the back row, third from the left

17/-. It's a good job I wasn't married then! There were two million unemployed and big fellows with all their limbs in the queue who couldn't find a job, and when I got to the counter the clerk was asking me, "Have you worked since you last signed?" That's what they used to ask you! "Have you been genuinely looking for work?" Then they brought out another dodge with a notebook. You had to take it round workshops and get them to sign to say that you'd been looking for work. There were some sad cases who were forced to do this.

Two years after my stay at Mosley Hill I was back there and had to see a woman specialist at Parliament Street. She sent me to a doctor at Broadgreen Hospital, Liverpool, for cosmetic surgery - but no-one had told me that. The doctor said he couldn't follow my records and asked if I knew who had passed me for the army. This was in the early 1950s! "You were young, weren't you?" he said. "What made you join?" I said I had wanted to see what was going on, and anyway things weren't too good at home and I thought I would be one less to keep. Eventually he explained what I was there for and said, "I can do the job for you, but I suppose everybody knows you now, don't they?" In other words, it was better to leave it after all those years but he would do it if I wanted. I told him I had agitated about my wounds but never got anywhere and he said, "You will do now because I'm putting you on the full 100%."

"Thank you very much, sir," I said. "You're the first one that's done anything for me since I came out of the army." That was about thirty-five years after I was wounded!

Post War Jobs

After the war I got a job at Burgess's Dairy on Gartside Street, Deansgate, driving horses and delivering milk from a two-wheeled float, then collecting the milk from the station. The dairy was tiled in white and stood where the new law courts are today, close to the old children's hospital. The stables were on Wood Street and when they were unloaded the horses would leave the dairy of their own accord and go back there, dray and all. It was a seven day a week job but I liked working with horses and they had some lovely animals. My favourite was a strawberry roan which I nursed like a baby. Mr Burgess was a big man who looked like a farmer, but mean - he wouldn't pay decent wages at all. He had a lot of young girls working for him and on his wagon was the message, "3,000 young healthy cows!"

However, I got on well with him. One Saturday afternoon when I returned to the shop after making my deliveries his wife said to me, "I'm glad you've come, Mick. I want you to take Mr Burgess home." "Home?" I said. "He's not drunk again!"

She said, "Is he ever sober?" I pointed out that I only had one arm and that it would be difficult to manage him and drive the cart but she said, "I couldn't trust anyone else with him. He likes you."

"Yes," I said, "but he won't give me any more ****ing money! I keep on asking him!"

But when I followed her into the back room where he was stretched out in an armchair he said, "We'll see you all right for this." He could hardly walk so we put a seat inside the float and a chain across to strap him to the churns of milk so he

Hard times: soup for the wives and children of ex-servicemen in Manchester, February 1921

wouldn't fall out and off I went with him to his beautiful big house in Broughton. I think he was an alcoholic - he drank spirits and I must have made at least three or four trips like this. His wife was such a puny little woman I don't know how she managed him. He had two sons working at the dairy who would ask me how I had gone on with him, and when I enquired why they didn't take him home they said, "Can't drive a horse!"

Another job I had was as a steam gauge regulator on regular nights at the Premier rubber heel place owned by Phillips's on Dantzic Street. The Dyers pub was near the Premier, opposite Smith's boneyard and "Paddy Jeff's" tripeworks. I remember seeing the tripe oozing through the wrapper bags, maggots and all! For a time I used to turn up for identity parades at Minshull Street police station too, but then I stopped bothering because you didn't get paid. When I lived in Mayor Street I had charge of a slaughterhouse for Stockdale's, who had many shops in the Manchester area. The keys were left with me and when the beasts came down I opened up the premises so they could be knackered.

They only slaughtered sheep in Mayor Street as there was no room for large animals. A knife was stuck into the throat and the blood flowed on to the floor - it was fairly easy to kill a sheep. I saw pigs being slaughtered in the Cheshire farmyards and that was much less pleasant. They would drag the pig by a rope round its jaw to a man with a large maul, the sort used to hammer down flagstones. He would hit it on top of the head to daze it, then they would slit it up the belly, gut it and throw it into a vat of boiling water. Next they'd string it up by its back legs, get the scrapers on it and it would be clean as a new pin within minutes. With horses, the vet put the humane killer against the forehead, hit it with his palm and the horse was shot off its feet in a flash. A cane was then raked inside the wound and into the animal's brain. In general, the modern methods of killing are much more humane.

I had a six-year-old seen off like this at Dean & Wood's in Bradford. Its fetlocks were worn and it was lame - I didn't do that to it, the people I lent it to did that. It was a good animal too. Dick Spencer, the butcher at Dean & Wood's, said to me when he was cutting it up, "Do you want a bit off the loin? I'm having some." I couldn't have eaten the flesh for all the tea in China! "You don't know what's good for you," said Dick. "It's as tender as chicken. Cooked properly, you wouldn't know the difference."

On the Market

Then I decided to go on the market, buying fish as my old woman had done when I was a lad. I had an aunt known as Granny Lynch who had a fruit and veg stall too, at the bottom of Oak Street outside where Bruce Craven had his shop. Prices hadn't changed much since before the war: I could buy a box of Manx kippers for 1/3d to 1/9d and sell them at eight pairs for 1/- or three-halfpence a pair. You could make a living out of two boxes of them then. There would be about 52 pairs

The Rising Sun, a popular market pub on Swan Street

of kippers in a box and we used to sell 20 boxes a day on Hillkirk Street market. It was a cheap feed for a big family. They'd say, "We can't eat all them," and I'd say, "What you can't eat you can make the fire with; they're good firelighters." You could buy three pounds of Finnan haddock for a shilling; cod was twopence-halfpenny a pound and steaks of silver hake threepence a pound. Ice was used for storage - 1/6d worth of ground ice from the stores would keep a six-stone box of codfish for days. That's how the retail fish market used to work as well, but there was also a cold air stores in the side street at the back of the market. When the fishing at Fleetwood deteriorated the fish market declined and some of the barrow mob moved in to take over but it didn't pay.

All the cafes had special hours for market days - the whole area was crowded and everybody seemed happy. Beerhouses were open at 5.00am when you could get a rum and coffee and a seat by the fire, and all the surrounding pubs were open as well. The George & Dragon wasn't popular with market folk but they used to go in the Bay Horse in Thomas Street and Bob Perry's (the Wheatsheaf) in Whittle Street, a Double Diamond house. The Rising Sun on Swan Street never shut - you could have a night's kip in there if you didn't mind the rats running under the forms and all over the place. The old-fashioned hawkers drank every penny they earned and their wives would come down to the market on a Monday morning. I'd say, "I haven't seen him," and the wife would shriek, "The bastard, I'll kill him! He's never been home all weekend! The kids is there! They've had nowt to eat! I've not paid the rent!" He'd been in the Rising Sun all weekend, supping! I'd go in and say, "Your wife's outside with a big knife," and he'd get nervous and ask, "Where is she? Where is she?"

Jack Bithell, who had the Glue Pot (the Prince of Wales) on Edge Street, kept a big green parrot on the bar in a wire cage. He'd offer to buy a drink for anyone who could get it to talk and when he said to it, "How are you?" it would answer, "All right, Jack" straight away. But when anyone else tried it wouldn't say a word! They had a jackdaw which could talk at the Nelson on the corner of Oldham Road and Radium Street. The pub was kept by the same family for years. If that bird heard anyone say, "D'you fancy a game of crib?" it would fly out of its cage to the shelf where the cards were kept, pick some cards up in its beak and take them to the table! After a time they used to put it outside and it would shout and whistle at people going past. They'd all be turning round, wondering who was calling them.

Another pub used by the market people was the Gaping Goose (the Shudehill Hotel). It was a big place shaped like a semicircle on the corner of Miller Street and Shudehill. I've known friends of mine knock on the front door in the morning, hand the landlady a couple of rabbits and ask her to cook them for opening time. When we went in, we would all get a free meal. Of course, the rabbits would only cost them 1/6d each and they'd sell the skins for 1/- apiece.

Nobody really had their own territory at the market, you just queued up for a place. There used to be a row of barrows one behind the other from Oldham Street to Stevenson Square. The

The 'Glue Pot' on Edge Street in the 1950s

hawkers would be running in and out of the Wine Lodge in between serving customers and would be there until twelve o'clock at night, though the law said you hadn't to serve after eight o'clock. If your barrow was there longer than a certain time you could be prosecuted for obstruction, but all the police did was to count up and say, "One down to ten - you're done." To get round this people would periodically pick up their barrow, take it for a walk and put it down again. The fines were about 5/-, going up to £2 if you had a lot of offences. When they owed a lot of money, people would just go to Blackpool or Birmingham for a bit - they rarely caught up with you as long as you kept on the move.

The pitch for the "flower gazers" was on the front of Piccadilly where Littlewoods is now. There were no barrows there; they had big, heavy baskets with a strap round them which would go over their neck when they carried them away. They would set these out just like a shop window front but they weren't allowed to rest the baskets on the pavement, they were supposed to keep them right in the road. Some of them liked to have their baskets on the front, near the public, and if a copper came along and caught them resting their baskets on the pavements, they were done. Eileen Turner, who stands near Queen Victoria's monument, is the oldest in the town still selling in the old-fashioned way.

The market folk had their own language, which more or less followed the alphabet backwards. For example, one was "eno", seven "neves" and ten "net". You might hear them calling out a price like "neves 'n exis (7/6d) a score!" The fruit was auctioned at the wholesalers' rooms in Liverpool and the "chalks" or classes of fruit were 1, 2, 3, 4, 5 and "no chalks" - that meant it had no class and you had to bid for it. The barrow people would always buy some of the good fruit to put on top - not that they were generally trying to cheat the public but obviously they had to recoup their own losses. Doubtful oranges would be stuck against the back wall so that no-one could see daylight through them; if you could, this showed they were wasting and third rate. If you dropped oranges like these on the ground, a green powder would come out. Your mates would warn you off them by saying, "Keep away - they're corks."

Of course, things were different then - you could buy 20 boxes of oranges for £15 and you'd sell 5 or 10 boxes rapidly. We bought in smaller quantities and sold twice as much - you used to reckon that the faster you turned your money over, the more you sold because it was all fresh. If you had to keep stuff, it was no good. I wouldn't sell swedes or potatoes either - people would only buy them in

At the vegetable market in the 1920s

Flower gazers in Piccadilly, December 1930

small quantities because they wouldn't carry them home.

There were some real characters at the market in those days, all with their nicknames such as Chinner Connor, the Soldier and the Bear. Chinner's real name was Gilbert O'Connor and he got his nickname because he was a good fighter and used to say, "I'll chin 'em." The Soldier and the Bear were flower sellers. Rosie Granelli of the ice-cream family used to stand on Shudehill on a Saturday night and she also had a stall on Conran Street Market. I've sold her as many as thirty baskets of strawberries. If I could see we weren't going to sell them I knew that Rosie would have them - the Granellis were a big family and had the fridges to store them. One of her children was a priest and when he saw me he would say, "I don't think she wants any today."

I knew Rosie couldn't say no and I'd reply, "How do you know? I've not asked her yet." I would tell Rosie, "I've got rid of the rough stuff and kept the best behind for you," charge her, say, 2/- if I'd bought them for 1/3d, go back to my mate and tell him to put the rest of the strawberries to one side until later when I would take them up to her. The Granellis were the biggest ice-cream firm in Manchester at that time. A lot of the ice-cream places were around Jersey Street, Hood Street and Oldham Road and they had more than anyone.

There were a lot of Italians in the area then. Most of their parents had come here to do terrazzo floor laying and the mosaics for sacred monuments, while others sold chestnuts, did fiddling or sold ice-cream like the Granellis - there were a lot in the catering business. I remember John Valente, Bertalone, Joe Andrussi and Scappaticci who shared stables with me at one time; they were good people and very sociable.

Another famous family I was friendly with were the Hudsons, who lived in Jersey Street model dwellings. It had been a mill before being converted into living accommodation and you could still see the large iron pillars and whitewashed steps leading down to the street. When the dwellings were demolished the family moved into a large, six-bedroomed house opposite the Green Dragon. Jackie Hudson was a lightweight boxing champion and fought John Tarpey, an Irishman whose family ran a "kip" in Angel Meadow; he later went to America boxing. Jackie beat him twice. Tarpey was a car park attendant on Watson Street not long ago and Jackie Hudson finished up on the rifle range at Blackpool. His sister Clara has a barrow on Cannon Street today.

During the last war the market porter with the biggest barrow was Jimmy Winter, a big tall lad with a turn in his eye. He was so strong, everyone would be after him to take their stuff. He once carried a hundredweight bag of potatoes from Smithfield Market to the Old Cock in Stretford for a bet. It poured down all the way and the load would have been getting heavier all the time - an empty bag in those days could weigh as much as half a stone when it was wet. He made it, but he finished up in Withington Hospital with pneumonia.

Charlie Nicholls' wife Nora was a character. Charlie had a lot of horse lorries lined up near the clock on the fish market and she did a man's job driving a two-wheeled dray. I used to see her near Wood Street stables dressed like a man in knee-breeches and black clogs.

Of course there were people on the market who weren't as friendly or hard-working. One who was notorious was a Birmingham fellow who lived at the top of Angel Meadow. They called him the Bullock. He had a minerals shop near Whittle Street but it was a cover-up place for stolen goods. If you annoyed him he'd say, "If you're not careful, I'll wipe your nose for you," and this is what he did. He'd have a handkerchief round a potato knife with the pointed end upwards and he'd dig his victim right under the tender part of the nose with the point. Of course, out they'd go and people would wonder what had happened.

A "kip" in Angel Street

Tib Street was the place for buying animals and birds. The bird people would be out all week with lime sticks and boxes catching goldfinches and larks which they would put in cages and sell there on a Saturday. Some of the dog sellers did the same sort of thing. They would walk round the posh neighbourhoods with aniseed in the bottom of their trousers, picking all the good class dogs out. You knew where to go if you'd lost your dog in those days!

There wasn't much cheating on the barrows. The only way they could fiddle was a long time ago when they used disc scales hanging from a beam by three chains. It was possible to manipulate the beam and make it weigh as they wanted but people soon caught on and shouted, "Don't be fiddling it with your little finger!" The weights and measures people were dead keen on checking and restamping the weights every twelve months, but some people's weights hadn't been stamped for years and if the inspectors caught these barrow hawkers out they were booked. There was one fellow, though, Tommy from Middleton, who had some wooden weights which were black-leaded to look like metal ones. He would just use them occasionally to make the customers think they had value for money and shout, "I give bumping weight!" No wonder! The barrow boys must lose a lot of money with the modern scales unless they use the automatic ones. They're the best because they make money for you and no-one can argue.

Angel Meadow and the Dardanelles

Angel Meadow, on the other side of Rochdale Road from the market, was a rough slum area. All the houses were one-up, one down and the policemen walked in twos. On a Monday morning you'd see the police dishing summonses out and they wouldn't miss a door - everyone would get one! One of the barrow mob married the sister of a lad from there who was the only one I knew ever to have the cat twice - for living on a woman's body. I saw him tried twice at the sessions court at Minshull Street.

The only way you can recognise the Meadow now is by the Weavers [Beer House]. The old pub was a little place where all the prostitutes and rough characters went and opposite was Kane's lodging house, in a big former warehouse. Not far away was the lodging house run by the family of John Tarpey, the boxer, and further down on each side were ordinary houses and smaller lodging houses. At the bottom of the Meadow was the Muckman's pub (the Crown & Cushion) and on the right as you walked down were some flags called St Michael's Flags, where there used to be a church at one time. Then there was the women's home, Ashton House, at the bottom.

Further up Rochdale Road on Pilling Street Biesty's owned a stone warehouse which they ran as a lodging house. John Biesty had horses and a box cart and used to do contract work for the council as well. There was a grocer's shop inside the kip and

Barrow hawkers near Shudehill in 1920

if you lodged with him you had to spend your money in his grocer's shop, otherwise he'd give you your ticket. The boozer near there was the Balloon Vaults, a Walker & Homfray's house near Ludgate Hill, which was run by a fellow called Mick Mannion who used to dress in American style with a rodeo hat and belted waist. The bar had a long, high counter and he always vaulted over it - he never opened the flap. He had eight kids who were comical - when you looked over the bar you'd see them, some too young to walk, crawling about and Mick was there, laughing at them. In the window he always kept a photograph of Steve Donoghue, the jockey.

I used to go in the Holt Town Tavern on Mitchell Street, Ancoats, which was kept by one of Mick Mannion's sons. The pub was opposite the Salvation Army and Star Hall, and it had a singing room. Just a bit further down was the Falcon; Walter Downs was the landlord there for years. Pubs I used in the Meadow itself were the Harp & Shamrock and the Royal George, in the days when you drank from pint pots with blue rings round and there were spittoons full of sawdust all over the place. The sawdust was bought by the bag from old fellows who used to come round with handcarts.

Another rough area near where I lived in Chapel Street, Ancoats, was nicknamed the Dardanelles. It was the bit around Lomas Street, Stanley Street, Sparkle Street and Chapel Street. The local pub was a Chesters house called the Shepherd and all the rough characters used to go in a side vault called the Carrot Yard which was supposed to be a women's room. A lad called Billy Green married one of the daughters; later he kept the Vauxhall on Rochdale Road. There were about four houses on one side of the street where the Shepherd was, three on the other and then you went down a flight of steps into Lomas Street. On a Saturday night when they'd got a few drinks in, the word would go round, "There's murder in the Dardanelles," and everybody would go to watch the fun. When the police got a call from there they used to have to strap the women to a two-wheeled stretcher to get them to the nick!

Two notorious characters who came up there from the Meadow were a pair of barrow hawkers, Crutchy Burns and his wife Maggie. They lived in Long Street, Ancoats, when I knew them. They were both red-haired and did more fighting than selling - one wrong word and there'd be carrots and vegetables flying in all directions. After Crutchy died Maggie lived with one of her daughters who had a grocer's shop on Brook Street near the Medlock pub. She was a nice, brown-haired girl married to one

Hard times. A Salvation Army mobile canteen with cheap dinners for the poor in Strangeways

of the flower sellers from town and later on they lived three doors from me in Fallowfield. But the parents were villains!

One Saturday dinner time when I lived in Wesley Street I called into the Crown & Sceptre, a Threlfalls house at the top of Chapel Street, on my way home. It was a sunny day and when I went in Crutchy Burns was there, wearing a straw cady. Everybody was quiet as he surged up to the bar and the landlord refused to serve him. "Why?" said Crutchy. "What have I done?"

"It's what you haven't done," the landlord replied, "and if you don't get out I'll call the police." I could see there was going to be some fun so I stood at the back out of the way.

"Well, you'll serve nobody else," snarled Crutchy as he took his crutch, swept all the beers off the counter with it and hopped outside. When I went out he had his back to the wall and his crutch upside down in his hand, threatening anyone who came near.

Hard Times

Conditions were pretty terrible for those who couldn't get work, right from when I came out of the army up to the thirties. A married man with children who was receiving a pension had to get his life certificate signed twice a year at the police station, but he couldn't go alone - he had to take his wife and children with him to prove they were all still living! It was a good life for the minority only. People were so poor that they couldn't find a halfpenny for a car ride and the authorities had patrols on the streets watching that you weren't doing sideline jobs anywhere. I've seen fellows being chased through the streets by them.

The workhouses were shocking, too - I went in the one at Crumpsall once to visit someone. It had brick walls with a green distemper wash, dim lights and stone steps. The inmates wore cord suits, tweed caps, grey army metal-buttoned shirts and big heavy Bluchers. Everybody knew a person out of the "dungeon" - they were branded. The inmates at Crumpsall and Withington, which also had a bad reputation, were made to work out at the farms, and they had to walk it. Then they had to go round with handcarts selling firewood to shops, they had to chop firewood inside the place and they were sent out to serve in shops and houses, anything to claw money out of them. Men and women were separated, they didn't stay as a family.

Any handouts to people on poor relief were given in kind, never in money. They might get loaves of bread or, if they had to go to a shop, a food ticket which could only be exchanged at places run by the pals of the Board of Guardians. The guardians used the system to make business for their own class.

Cheap accommodation was much in demand and there were working men's lodging houses all over the show. As soon as a shop came empty somebody would put a couple of curtains up to the window and they were in business. I never used them, but the best in our area was Walton House on Harrison Street, near Pollard Street, Ancoats. I lived in Tame Street directly opposite it when I was a boy. There were 740 beds with individual cubicles and commercial travellers would put up there before they'd pay the money charged by the hotels. It had every facility you needed:

Walton House in the 1980s

baths, washing was undertaken, food could be bought inside the building, there was a strongroom where you could leave money and valuables and get a receipt, and if you were working late or on shifts you could pay for a knocker-up. The only charge was 6/6d for a bed and you could come in at any hour provided you behaved yourself. But it took all the work in the world to get in there. When you applied for a vacancy they wanted to know every little detail: where you had come from, where you'd been before that, whether you were married, how many children you had, where you worked. Before they would give you a room or put you on the waiting list they'd say, "Call in again and we'll see what can be done for you."

Next to this hostel was the Tame Street Tramp Ward, which was a very different kettle of fish. It accommodated down-and-outs but after 10.00pm they were only admitted if accompanied by a policeman and there was plenty of fun when they came back half drunk after that time. They'd be shouting and swearing, kicking on the doors and demanding to be let in, and the staff would shelter behind the heavy wooden doors until the law arrived. One man I remember quite well was on the roads in summer but he came every year as soon as winter set in and stayed for the duration of the bad weather. He was a tinker and rolled up with a big, four-wheeled, home-made cart stacked with kettles, pots and pans, all bright and shining new. They had to open the large yard gates to let him in. People entering the Tramp Ward were supposed to do a day's work before they were free to leave but it was common to see them climbing over the wall and running away down Tame Street to escape "the task", once they'd had a good night's sleep and a meal. A small residential staff lived in; they chopped firewood from disused railway sleepers and went round the streets with a handcart, selling the bundles to shops and wholesalers.

There were quite a few timber firms in the area and Southern's in Store Street made packing cases as well. They formed a partnership under the name Southern & Darwent and their place at Collier Street, Liverpool Road, is still going. Parker's timber yard was off Cannel Street, going towards Ancoats Hospital and closer to the mill area. So was the aerated water factory of Bratby & Hinchcliffe. Then there were the mills themselves, belonging to firms like Bennett's, McConnel & Kennedy's, Lawson's, Bannerman's and many more. Shaw, Jardine & Co were on Butler Street just past the old Angel. Steamers used to come to the dock in Ducie Street, each pulling three barges behind it loaded with bales of cotton.

At the top of the steep hill called Stony Brow, near Shillinglaw & Hulme's, was the firm of Thomas Hassall, drysalters, where my brother worked for forty years. They were the only drysalters in England and supplied rock salt, moss litter and all kinds of things. Our kid drove the horses. He travelled miles, as far as Poynton and Macclesfield, and would come in at all hours of the night. Later he transferred to the motors - they had three big Leylands. When I said he was wasting his time he'd say, "Well, I've worked nowhere else and we'll be all right if anything happens to the old man." Thomas Hassall wasn't married and he'd promised to leave all his people something when he died.

Thomas Hassall's drysalters. My brother worked here for over forty years

Well, eventually he had to have one of his legs off and the firm finished but they were very disappointed with what they got. I think our kid got £50 for his forty years' service!

Pub Life - and Death

There was a pub on nearly every street and I've been in most of them in my time. A lot had entertainment as well in those days. The George & Dragon (now the Band on the Wall) on Swan Street was kept by a fellow called Tyson who was often in trouble with the police. He had been in the Coldstream Guards and was a bit of a tearaway, but he lost more fights than he won. I was told that Leslie Stuart, the composer of "Soldiers of the Queen" and "Lily of Laguna", played the piano at the George & Dragon in his spare time. He was the organist at St John's, Salford and at the Church of the Holy Name, Oxford Road, but that was before my time.

Tommy Brown, nephew of the policeman "Pigeon", had the Devonshire and his brother Georgie Brown had the Queens, Queens Road and the Top Kings on Oldham Street. Another friend of mine who had a pub was Tim Carlisle, who kept the Pack Horse on Oldham Road. At one time he sold sheet music in Blackpool. I can picture him now with his straw cady on doing turns on stage or singing in pub concerts. His sister Elsie was one of the leading female singers in the twenties and thirties and her son still works for the BBC.

Landlord of the Moulders Arms on Heyrod Street was John McDonough, my platoon sergeant in B Company, 7th Platoon. He was only about five feet four inches tall but very smart. He got stripped twice when I was with him and got his stripes back again. I think he enlisted as a territorial on the outbreak of war - as far as I know he was never a regular soldier - but he carried on at the same pace, regardless of the shells falling all about us. I remember him saying to me, "If your number's on it, you'll get it." He saw action in the Middle East, Gallipoli, France and Flanders and came through without a scratch. John was a nice fellow who never used any bad language himself and didn't like to hear it used in the pub. His wife's brother, "Blind Henry", lived with them and John looked after him as he wasn't able to work because of his disability. After hours drinking was rife in the twenties and thirties and you could always get in the Moulders - the door was left ajar and policemen were regulars. I've seen them drunk as fools in there often. The last time I was

Tim Carlisle's pub, the Pack Horse on Oldham Road

John McDonough's Moulders Arms

in Johnny Sands had drawn a horse called Dastur in the Irish Sweepstake - everybody in the pub bought him a drink and he went around paying their bills for them! I think the Moulders got its name from Hetherington's heavy engineering works nearby. The street used to be full of terraced houses, the boys' club and a girls' club next door facing the pub and further down the back of Joe Whalen's garage. He started with an old Model T Ford van and a contract with the "Daily Herald" and finished up one of the biggest haulage contractors delivering newspapers in Manchester. Today most of the houses on Heyrod Street have been knocked down and there is only the block with the Moulders left.

There was a place called Harry's Bar, a lock-up pub on Newton Street which attracted people from far and wide. The window was boarded to a height of three or four feet, with glass at the top and curtains. There was only one entrance with the bar to one side and the toilet at the top of a flight of stairs facing you - if someone hadn't shut the door you could see them performing as you went in! There were no women allowed in the pub and all the characters used to collect in there. I always knew the manager as Ginger Foster because he worked in the fish market before he got the job there. He might come at nine o'clock in the morning and you'd see the curtains and go in and get served. Then he might come at six or seven at night, people would make their way down there and all of a sudden he'd look at his watch and say, "Come on, drink up. I've had enough. I'm going home." This would drop on you like a load of bricks and you couldn't make him change his mind. "You're getting no more so you might as well go," he'd say. "I've got to be up early." Someone might ask him, "Why, what time are you getting up?" and the reply would be, "Well, it all depends how I feel"!

Buller Whatmough's on Malaga Street stood near the second highest chimney in Lancashire. It was several hundred feet high and stood on railway land towering above the little terraced houses. There was no factory near it, just parked lorries and I never saw smoke coming out of the top. Around the base was a wall about eight feet high, so it was fairly easy to climb this and gain access to the ladders running up the side of the chimney. On weekend evenings in summer the regulars at Buller Whatmough's would congregate in the street looking up at the monster; it was a common thing for men to climb the stack for a bet. This pub had closed by 1930 and another one that went early on was the Blink Bonny on Port Street, which was taken over in the thirties by the Rices, the ice-cream family, to use as a freezing house. The building is still there today and you can see the words "Rices Ices" in the doorway.

Our family used to gather in the Crown & Anchor on Hilton Street at Whit Week to meet the

Harry's Bar, on the corner of Newton Street and Dale Street

parents. There was no entertainment there, it was just a plain drinking pub but it suited us. Sam Marshall, the landlord, was an uncivilised fellow, though. He had a deaf wife and used to call her all sorts of terrible things in the hearing of the customers. He committed suicide in the end and nobody was sorry.

Just opposite the pub was one of the best cafes in the area, run by a fellow called Tom. It was open Sundays and was very cheap with just tables and long forms inside, but people came miles for his fat cakes, special pots of tea or bacon and eggs. Round the corner from there were the premises of the Buxton lime firms and on Brewer Street was "Donkey Read's", where they made the stone for stoning steps.

Not far away were two private betting clubs, the Prince of Wales and the Ellesmere. The only legal way of betting then was if you were a member of a club and there used to be a policeman around that area between Faraday and Warwick Streets all day long. If you walked past him showing a "one o'clock" in your pocket he arrested you for gambling right away! Everyone knew his number - B11 - and he had them running in all directions.

When we weren't boozing we used to go to watch the cases in the police courts in Minshull Street. There was a window high up at one end of the entrance hall as you went in and the policeman used to open it and shout through it at the top of his voice, "Separation cases this way!" or "Bastard cases this way!" Sometimes the "customers" were prostitutes - the area around Ardwick Barracks was full of them and they used to parade around the park where the railings are today. The soldiers used to call them "green linnets". Most of them lived in a lodging house on Manor Street and when you went past at night you could hear them screaming at each other in the basement - it was usually over a man.

Another way of passing time was to go and listen to the speakers in Stevenson Square on a Sunday. One, Jimmy Rochford, started as a Communist and ended up as a Catholic. Another called Kilgarrif had been a cruiserweight boxer in the navy and was a Communist. He came from Openshaw and threw a red flag round the Shah of Persia's neck when he went through there in his carriage. Scottie Matthews was well educated and a good speaker. He began selling the Melbourne racing system, guaranteed to pick three winners a day - we all bought it as kids. Every Sunday night after the meeting was over the speakers would go in the Crown & Anchor with the collection to see how much they'd got.

Quite a bit later I had an

Buller Whatmough's beerhouse and shop next door in 1912

For Scouring and Cleaning Doorsteps, Windowsills, Flags, &c.

NOTHING EQUALS

☞ **READ'S**

DONKEY BRAND

Each Genuine Tablet bears our Registered Trade Mark. . . . .

REFUSE IMITATIONS!

Sold by Grocers, Ironmongers, &c., everywhere.

SOLE PROPRIETORS AND MANUFACTURERS:

EDWARD READ & SON,
Brewer Street, Port Street, MANCHESTER.

interest in a pub myself - I had £350 invested in the Bowling Green, Grafton Street, Chorlton-on-Medlock, which was run by Joe Stanley, a friend of mine. I was associated with the pub for about eight years, not serving but doing the detective work! It was a gold mine once he'd got rid of the rubbish; after that the regulars were as good as gold if handled right. The only trouble we had was with two brothers who lived in Dover Street. What a dive that was! It was said in the neighbourhood that they had kicked their own father to death. We wouldn't have them in the pub, though I used to buy gear from them occasionally on the black market. One of the brothers had a business where all the "hook and eye" ("Who can I tap for a nicker?") merchants used to go. He'd be in with them, buying the swag or fencing it for them. The plain clothes fellows soon shifted him!

One sad thing that happened in the twenties was a killing, to which I was a witness, in a little Chesters house on St Andrews Street. The Globe was only a tiny pub with two steps up to the front door and if there were six people in the vault you were choking. The landlord, Jim George, had two daughters; one of them married Bob Sanderson, a lad I knew who was a pig-slaughterer at Goodwin's on the corner of Every Street and had fought at Gallipoli with the Manchester Regiment. The other daughter, Irene, used to help her father in the pub.

On this Saturday night Tommy Kelly and I had been to a Hyde Road football match and we'd only been in the Globe for about ten minutes when in came Bill Taylor, the brother of Tom, who had pinched the barrel with me from outside the Manchester Brewery. Bill had obviously woken up out of a drunken sleep and his hair was standing on end and his eyeballs sticking out of his head. "Give us a pint of bitter," he said to Irene and Jim shouted to him from the kitchen to go home because he'd had enough.

"Just give me one," Bill pleaded and Jim said, "You're not in a fit state to have any - if the police see you I'll get into trouble. Go and sleep it off and you can have what you want later." He came out to the bar and Bill got hold of an empty pint pot from the bar and went to crack him with it. The daughter ran to a drawer and pulled out a German bayonet which someone had given her as a souvenir. He was half turned as she stuck it in him and he fell backwards, pushing it into his back as he slumped to the floor. We ran out for the police. There was a police station at the bottom of Fairfield Street, someone ran to tell them and they were there in two minutes. By that time Bill was dead and a horse ambulance came later and shifted the body. Irene was brought up for trial at Strangeways and Tommy and I were witnesses. The trial went on for weeks and weeks but she got away with it in the end on the grounds that it was self-defence.

I had a photo of Irene and could have had money from newspaper reporters for it. One came to our house when I was out and asked my mother about it. Before he called back I mentioned it to Jim and he asked me to do him a favour and not let them have it. "I don't want her exposed any more than she is being," he said, so when the newsman came back I told him I'd lost it. Jim offered to give me whatever money they mentioned but I wouldn't have it - he was a nice old fellow.

The Crown & Anchor on Hilton Street - where the Stevenson Square speakers counted their takings

Hawking Adventures

As times got worse I started up on my own. You could go to the Ministry of Pensions in Dickinson Street and apply for money out of the King's Fund. I needed a fourteen hands pony, a cart, scales and stock to set myself up. They gave me all sorts of forms to fill in and then there was an interview at the Town Hall. Mary Kingsmill-Jones was on the committee who interviewed me. They were very brusque with you at the Pensions place and would call the police at the first sign of trouble, but in the end I got what was called a "commutation of pension" allowance - in other words I gave up 10d from my pension and they allowed me £40. I'm still paying the 10d - now 10p - today! Even then they didn't give you cash. Vic Towers next door had a light bay pony and a cart which he let me have for £25 and I had to take them the bill for this, and for the scales and stock when I got them.

At first I worked round the mill areas of Shaw and Royton as there weren't two wealthier places in the country before the cotton slump came. Then working people with shares in local firms saw all their life savings go and big shareholders lost a fortune. At seven o'clock at night the towns were just like evacuated cities - all the mills had the blinds pulled down, the machinery had been sold and most people were on the dole, so they stayed indoors.

I served two brothers who had lost their jobs like this. They lived on Lees Road and the lady from the toffee shop next door was a casual customer. She lived with her sister as she suffered very badly with rheumatism and was confined to a wheelchair. One Thursday I called in and she asked if I had been next door. "Not yet," I replied. "I'm going there next and then I'll have my lunch across the road in the White Hart."

"I can usually hear them knocking about," she said, "but it's been very quiet for some time." In those days all you did was knock on the door and walk in and I was a bit surprised when I went to the brothers' house and there was no shout of, "Come in. How are you?" but I went in anyway. One of them was sitting in the chair with his head down and at first I thought he was asleep, then I saw the large pool of blood on the floor. The poor devil had cut his throat! I called the lady from the toffee shop in and ran to ask the landlord of the pub to telephone the police. When the ambulance came, they told me he was dead.

Rhodes was another part of my beat and we were getting ready to start one morning when we were approached by a nicely dressed gentleman wearing a straw cady and carrying a walking stick. We got into conversation and he ordered a box of Jaffas, one of apples and one of bananas. I thought, "We'll finish before we've

At Smithfield Market

started here!" He directed us to a big house up the road and told us to say that Mr Parkinson had sent us and that we were to be paid. A maid came to the door, took the message and returned a few minutes later with the manager of the place. "Who sent you?" he asked. The man was still in sight, so I pointed him out. "Oh, take no notice of him," he said. "It's a mental home, this."

About this time Clara Hudson said to me, "Hey, Mick, the Arabs (our name for the market lads) are all going to Blackpool on the rock job." Some were already doing well there, another lad called Christmas Eve (Steve Ashton) was going and Chinner Connor, who had worked with me a time or two, said he would go if I would, so I decided to try my luck. When I arrived all the lads from Manchester were there and we would meet outside the New Inn near Woolworths when business was over. Before Woolworths was built we sold rock, papers and all sorts from baskets on the pavement, but afterwards they complained about us causing an obstruction and the police would arrive in taxi cabs to grab us and take us to the nick, baskets and all. We were harassed so much that we had to leave in the end. Some of the Arabs owed £200 in fines and wouldn't pay, so they had to return to Manchester and elsewhere. Harold Cavanagh was the only one who stuck it out and the last time I went to Blackpool he was still there. I went backwards and forwards for many years to see a mate of mine who had been blinded in the Great War. He married Cissie Russell, the widow of Paddy McGrath who had played full back for Manchester City and was killed in the war. After a time in St Dunstan's they fixed him up with a basket-making workshop at the back of his house in Ruth Avenue, Marton and he did quite well - you could always make a living in Blackpool.

In those days you made money any way you could. Once I found out that the Tramp Ward would pay for railway sleepers I started on that job - it was easy to drive on to the railway sidings and the sleepers were stacked all over the place. On my first visit to Tame Street Tramp Ward I dealt with a Mr Jones, a Welshman with an accent so strong that I could hardly understand him. They had a weighing machine in the back of the building and he gave me thirty-six shillings for just over a ton of wood. I thought to myself, "That's all right; I'm going back again." Then I met a chap who told me that the Central Hall, Oldham Street, would pay thirty shillings a ton and that they also had a place in Hood Street at the back of the Daily Express building. This was a similar kind of hostel to Tame Street and the Salvation Army hostels but it was run by the Methodist Church. The man in charge was the Reverend Mr Carpenter and one morning I called to see him in Central Hall. He said he would have as many sleepers as I could provide and pay me thirty-five shillings a ton for them, so the next job was to find some weights. I lived in Wesley Street at the time and was stabling just across the road, close to a scrap iron yard. Jackie Garrity shared the stables with me; he had a big draught horse and we were running a coal round. I thought the firewood business would fit in

Mick (front right) with his younger brother, John Farrell, and two friends, Percy Davies and Jack Green, in Blackpool. They called themselves 'The Fornicating Four'!

Outside the market, near Edge Street

nicely with what we were doing, so one morning I said to him, "I've got a job selling railway sleepers to a minister at Central Hall and I want to pinch a bit of weight. Have you got any spare?"

"I've got a lot there," he said. "Help yourself." By the time I had finished I had 56lb and 100lb weights on the front of the lorry, covered over with a horse rug! I went to the railway sidings, piled the sleepers on top and then went to Hood Street with my loot.

One good beat I had was near the Queens Road depot on Johnson Street. A lot of wealthy Jews lived round there, mostly furriers and diamond merchants who couldn't speak a word of English - there were Russians and all sorts. I would have to take a big tray of samples into the house and a notebook with the prices written down, and they'd jabber away in their own language. They made their own wine and would buy a whole barrel of grapes from us, or a box of bananas or Jaffas. Chinner and I made sure we looked stylish for that one - we had tailored suits.

A friend of mine tried all sorts of dodges to earn a living. At one time he set himself up as a commission agent in the end house of Lever Street - quite illegally. He was a bit nervous about going to the authorities because he was a deserter from the navy! Then he got a team of men smashing car batteries into powder and sold the result as blacklead. When he was hawking with me he used to work the big houses in Cheshire and elsewhere selling washleathers. A firm in Nelson supplied him by post and the first thing he did was to cut each one in two to increase his profit that way. It's a good job the owners of the houses didn't know how he made the leathers so nice and soft - he once asked me to save my urine so he could soak them in it! He did all right for himself too - he finished up with a betting shop, a cafe in Cambridge Street and a big house at St Anne's.

When things got really bad because of the slump I went to the rich areas round Cheshire and North Wales: Wrexham, Chester, Northwich, Winsford and Mere Corner. The Ridings, the hire purchase people, were good customers and would buy a box of twelve dozen bananas from me all at once, but I used to sell to farmers and golf clubs as well as to private families. I had a posh turnout for that: a horse with white stockings, a cart with rubber tyres and cane shafts and painted on the back my name in gold, a bunch of bananas and the slogan, "Buy more fruit." At the Swan on Bucklow Hill they would lend me a tray to take round samples and I used to call at the Smoker and the Nags Head on my way to Northwich. I lodged there at a beerhouse on Church Road, where the landlord, Henry Wilding, bred Dalmatians.

I made some good sales at the Bleeding Wolf in Northwich - but I lost a customer as a result. My mate would take a box of haddock in and I'd take a box of kippers, ready opened with nice waxed paper on top and the oil from the kippers oozing through it. We'd put the boxes on the counter, order two pints and then start chewing a kipper each. One day the pub was full of Irish haymakers and one of them noticed us. I told him, "They're so good, these, they're cooked when raw." It was true; with a well-cured pair you could tear the flesh off and eat it. You'd often see people chewing kippers in a beerhouse. Anyway, he bought six pairs for a shilling and we were away - they all wanted some. You

Horse transport and Manchester warehouses in the 1920s

could always sell a box of kippers in a boozer. I went back the next week but when I called at a local farm the farmer complained that I had served half his customers and told me not to come back!

The only time I left the hawking for long was during the Second World War when I got conscripted for work of national importance. I said, "I've never worked for national importance!"

"Well," said the man, "you can work now!"

Things were bad on the market; the blockade was on and there was only a certain allocation of fruit coming through so a lot of us took jobs and mine was with English Steel. I was in luck because I knew the security policeman, Frank Brown (better known as "Pigeon" to a lot of people) and he said, "If you want to get out, you're all right," so I could come and go as I pleased. I'd often have a drink with him in the Lord Wolseley on Ashton Old Road coming off shift at ten o'clock. He was a big, smart fellow and a great pal of mine. I first got in with him one August Bank Holiday at Didsbury Horse Show when he was in the Mounted Police and we were still friendly when he retired.

Horse Culture

In my young days all transport, food deliveries and everything depended on horses and there were plenty of vets in Manchester. There was one not far from the British Rail Club in Store Street. Turn right out of the club, go to the first street on the right and Joe's Garage stands not far from the site of it - Ward's Veterinary Surgeons. It was a large practice with stables and a house, which he had in addition to his big private residence at the top of North Road, Clayton. Jimmy O'Donnell, the greengrocer I worked for as a young lad, kept his pony there. There was another vet who looked after the police horses called Locke. His premises were in Grosvenor Street, Chorlton-on-Medlock, opposite Creamer's lodging house.

There was a smithy on every street corner and there was fierce competition. One would say, "I'll do it for seven-and-a-tanner all round with pads," another would charge six-and-a-tanner and a third a dollar. One of the biggest firms was Greaves & Faulkner's, who did the shoeing for a lot of large businesses in the city and also for the London & North Western Railway. Their premises were at the top of the arch in Travis Street, near the Star & Garter.

My smith was a fellow named Bob Wynne, who ran a business off Beswick Street, Ashton New Road. There were two shoeing smiths and a couple of stables, which I used at one time. Bob was a very good blacksmith who could also act as a vet and advise you about buying and selling horses. A good shoeing smith like him who had served an apprenticeship and had been in the game for a long time could save you a lot of money.

Corn shops were scattered all over the place too. I remember one on Cheetham Hill Road and another called Grange's at the top of Store Street. Mixed corn was seven-and-a-tanner a hundredweight but some people still couldn't - or didn't - feed their horses properly. One of

Manchester carters at Pomona Docks

these was getting in through the loft of my stable and stealing corn but I caught him, using an old wrinkle a farmer taught me. Horses are very keen over their food but they're very clever - you could throw a needle into a manger full of corn and come back to find the corn gone and the needle in the bottom of the empty manger. This time I cut a length of string up into little pieces until I had a big handful and mixed it in with my corn. Sure enough, there was string left in this fellow's manger but even when I showed him he tried to deny it so I told him to get out and take his horse with him!

Horses are marvellously clean animals; that nose piece moves around like a cushion, sorting out all the time. One I had would start in the middle when I filled the manger, moving the feed to one side, then give it one swish and the corn would go up the wall with the oats on top. Then it would start pulling it together in little lots before it ate, just like setting the table! They filter their drinking water through their teeth, too, and if you take a horse to a trough on a windy day it'll shake the water about with its nose until it gets rid of all the dust before it will start to drink.

I loved working with horses. I used to give each one of them a name - Tommy, Peggy or Annie - and put the names up over the stalls. At one time I had four horses in stables in McCormick Street, off North Porter Street. One was for me, one for my brother and two for hire. I charged eight bob a day for a turnout or a pound a week and its keep, but if you did that you had to go and make sure they were feeding it properly.

There was a barber called Charlie Crossley on North Porter Street and I was in there at nine o'clock one morning when a mate of mine came in looking the worse for wear. He admitted he was bad but said, "I'll have some more tonight," and when the barber had shaved him and cut his hair he gave him a food ticket!
"What's that?" said Charlie. "That's no good to me."

Putting a donkey through its paces

"Well it's money to me," said my mate and left him to it!

He was called Charlie too and he was always making merry. He got very, very fat and when he was coming home with me one day he leant forward and burst his trousers at the back. I'd pulled up at the Bridge, Heap Bridge, where a lot of the hawkers used to go, and he was missing for half an hour. I eventually found him sitting in the best room with the door shut, sewing up his trousers!

A day at the horse sales was always a good day out, but a drunken one! We used to go by train from Central Station to Chelford in Cheshire or from London Road Station to Crewe. The local sales were held at Bradshaw's in Manchester, opposite the Palace on Whitworth Street, and there was Smith's on Park Street, Cheetham Hill, but that was no good. Crewe was always worth going to as you could pick some good young stuff about five or six years old from the area round about Sandbach. For our job we wanted horses about 15.2 hands, or cobs, fourteen to fifteen hands high. After a while you got to know what to look for. Up to about eight years old you can tell their age by looking at their teeth; it's not a reliable guide after that. Then you look at the legs, the fetlocks, the loins, the back joints and from the hock down to see that it hasn't got windgall and hasn't sprained a tendon. (Windgall is a kind of spongy swelling on the inside of a horse's leg which makes the creature lame. It goes flat sometimes but when it gets full of fluid you've got to rest the horse.) Finally, you've got to check that the horse's knees aren't over-drawn as a result of it being worked too hard. When I went to the sales you could take the horse for a run but anyone using a whip was barred.

There were two ways of buying

a horse - with a "character" or on the open market. An auctioneer opening the bidding might say, "I'm selling this horse with a 'character'. It's sound in every way and will work in shafts or in chains, single or double." (It will go on the bit single-ringed or double-ringed.) "It goes to bed every night and sleeps on both sides." (Some horses won't lie down at all.) "Who'll put her in at five-and-twenty?" and the bidding would start. If the horse didn't turn out as promised you could take it back in a fortnight's time and get your money back. If you bought a horse on the open market you had to take pot luck and you knew you were buying all the trouble with it, so the bidding would start at a tenner.

I slipped up once when I bought one from a dealer called Squire Kirkham of Hawthorn Farm in Urmston. It was advertised as a light bay, sixteen hands high and only six years old, so I went up to see it one Monday. It looked a lovely animal, he only wanted sixteen quid for it and he offered to get it shod for me, so I bought it. I went back two days later to collect the bay and tied it to the back of the cart, thinking that was sixteen quid well spent, but the next morning as I was jogging down Oldham Road a pal named Jimmy Martin shouted to me, "Your horse is nodding forward." It was running lame on its offside leg. I took it back to the stable, changed horses and took it to the smithy later on in the day. Bob Wynne pared the hoof and found it had a corn; you can't cure a horse with a corn so I took it back to Urmston.

He offered me a little rough-haired pony of about fourteen hands but that was no good to me - I was doing about forty miles a day all round Cheshire. I told him I would fetch the RSPCA if he didn't give me my money back. He refused, so I saw Murphy, the Irish RSPCA inspector on the market. They'd had a lot of trouble with that particular man selling lame horses, so he told me he would have a word with him and then I was to go back and say he'd send the police in if I had any trouble getting my money. This time I got it!

The RSPCA inspectors were very keen then, especially one Irishman. If he saw a horse shivering he'd be there right away, feeling under the saddle to see if it had a sore or anything. He used to stand at the junction of Stretford Road and City Road, Old Trafford, where there was a water trough. All the carriers used to pass that way - Jimmy Hancock's, Thomas Maiden's and so on - and he used to wait there to see if they were overloaded. As they pulled in to water the horses he would be ready for them!

One good buy I got was a rogue horse from a pig farmer in Droylsden. It was a really good animal - they usually are. I had a strawberry roan this man fancied and he pestered the life out of me, offering to exchange it for the one in his field. It was a big, rough-looking creature with its coat standing on end and it looked starved to death because it had been out all the time. I said, "It wants clipping - it would take twelve months to get the hair off it," and I saw its ears go back. Horses aren't too safe then and you have to be cautious of them. Some time later he still hadn't found a buyer and I said I'd give him a fiver for it to stop him moithering. There was nothing wrong with it except that when you came to clean it or brush it under its stomach it would jump about and you couldn't do a thing with it. That's why he sold it.

Well, I put it in a lorry and gave it all the long journeys, so that it was doing forty miles a day and sixty when I went round Rochdale and Oldham on a Thursday. It was out a full twelve hours and at the market

A busy corner: Market Street and Cross Street in 1935

at 5.30am. At first it used to jump in the collar when you shouted to it, but the work slowed it down and I treated it very gently, calming it down bit by bit and cutting down the oats in its feed - they make a horse very fresh if you use too many. Eventually it became a really good worker and looked a picture when I had finished grooming it. The farmer even tried to buy it back but I told him it wasn't for sale!

Nearly all working horses were gelded then - the streets wouldn't have been safe otherwise. To show you what I mean I'll tell you the story of John Quayle's donkey which was kept in our stables. It was a full Billy (not gelded) and a picture of an animal with ears nearly eighteen inches high, black, with a cross on its back just like a crucifix. Quayle had the donkey for years and worked the Clayton area of the city with it, then decided to bring it to the donkey show at London Road Fire Station on May Day. At one point there were ten firemen trying to hold it, and it was reared up on its hind legs with its penis trailing on the ground - and with all those people about, including the Lady Mayoress!

Another time it was left near where the tramcars stopped with a cart minder called Joe Irving. All the dealers paid him half-a-crown a week and he would mind their carts to see that nothing was pinched while they went for their meal. When I came back after my dinner I saw that there were potato sacks hung over the shafts. "What's the idea of the bags, Joe?" I asked.

"That dirty ****!" he replied. "It's disgraceful, with women and children getting off the trams. I'm embarrassed myself!" He had discreetly placed the bags to save the women from embarrassment and was most upset. After that, he refused to mind it any more!

The annual Donkey Parade at the Fire Station, 1931. The dignitaries are the Lady Mayoress, the Mayor and Mayoress of Salford and the Dean of Manchester

What's Left

This walk from Oldham Street, down Ancoats Lane and around parts of Ancoats Mick knew well was written just before the book was first published in 1985. In ten years more of the old landmarks have gone and so the walk was updated in the summer of 1995. The numbers refer to the map on the back cover.

Start from Piccadilly and walk up Oldham Street, On the right hand side is the Central Hall [1]. *Here I sold railway sleepers to a Methodist minister for use in their missions here and in Hood Street.* The Hen & Chickens [2] closed many years ago and in 1985 part of the building was in use as a discount warehouse. *Before the First World War the landlord here was called Foy. One of his daughters married the boxer, Boy McCormick and they later kept the Crown & Kettle on the corner of Oldham Road and Great Ancoats Street.* Today there is gap in the line of Oldham Street where the Hen & Chickens once stood, but you can still see a reminder of the pub - the word "Billiards" on the back wall.

The site of Affleck's store [3] is on the other side of Oldham Street. *They had a fleet of horses and vans and the drivers wore a livery consisting of maroon riding breeches, leggings, double-breasted coat and peaked cap.* The old Yates's butcher's and teetotal tavern [4] occupied 77 to 83 Oldham Street. *They sold Bosley beef and killed their own cattle. In the tavern you could get good soup and bread was in a wire netting case on the counter. All the dossers used to go in there from the hostels nearby.* Part of the premises were in use as a lighting shop in 1985, but you could still see the Yates's name in the doorway and the board for their butcher's shop at the back in Tib Street. Two bars now occupy the Oldham Street frontage.

Go back to the corner of Hilton Street, turn right and right again into Tib Street. At 39 Tib Street [5] was Walter Smith's shop. *I bought the canaries which I sold in Cheshire from this firm. Tib Street was always the place to buy cage birds or dogs.* No.39 is now a video shop, but the firm still has a shop further up Tib Street.

From Tib Street turn down Green Street (now Dorsey Street), left into Oak Street and right into Edge Street. On the corner of Hare Street is the Glue Pot [6], which was being used as a fashion shop in 1985. *This is where Jack Bithell had the talking parrot. The pub's proper name was the Prince of Wales but it was always known as the Glue Pot.*

Go back to Oak Street and turn left, then right into Whittle Street. On the corner is the Wheatsheaf [7]. *This was Bob Perry's pub. Bob was the brother of one of the market lads and this was always a pub popular with the market traders.*

From Whittle Street cross Oldham Street into Warwick Street. On the right, where the bus station is now [8], was the Ellesmere betting club. The building was pulled down a few weeks after this book was first published in 1985. The big building which is still standing on the other side of Warwick Street, on the corner of Lever Street, was the Prince of Wales betting club. Round the corner, on Lever Street, was the house [9] where Mick's friend had his commission agent's business.

At the end of Lever Street turn right at the Land o'Cakes on to Great Ancoats Street. On the next corner [10] was Zeltner's pork butcher's. *Their shop was smashed up during a wave of anti-German feeling in the Second War, just as the Gilberts' shop had been in the First War.*

Continue down Great Ancoats Street. Just before the canal, on your right, on the corner of Binns Place, is the Brownsfield Mill [11]. *Here A V Roe started manufacturing his aeroplanes shortly before 1915. I saw some of them in action in France.*

Cross the road and walk up Union Street (now Redhill Street). On the corner of Henry Street is McConnel's mill [12]. Note the date-stones on the Union Street and Henry Street entrances. *Our Nellie worked here and I used to take her dinner on my way back to school. I remember being terrified of the noise the first time I went and coming out teeming in sweat from the heat.*

Cross the footbridge over the canal from Henry Street. In 1985 this led into Dawn Street, formerly the continuation of Henry Street. All the old streets hereabouts have gone and a row of superstores covers the area. In 1985 you could walk along Allum Street and Fawcett Street, which came out on Great Ancoats Street opposite the White House pub, just about where the superstores entrance is now. Further along was John Street (later Fawn Street) and St Alban's Church and School [13], where Mick started his education. The "Toys R Us" store covers this site. What would Father Tim have said about that?

The White House [14] was always a bit of a white elephant. The Abercrombie on the next corner [15] did better, Next door to it was Sibbit's shop (S Wilson, Auto Scales in 1985, a butty bar in 1995) *and on the other side of Great Ancoats Street [16] stood the Scotch Heifer.* Continue along Great Ancoats Street to the corner of Mill Street. *On the corner of Mill Street was Paul Ryan's wringing machine shop [17]. People used to joke about there being a smash and grab raid there.*

To the left, across Mill Street was the site of Mill Street Industrial School [18]. *Ancoats Hospital is at the crest of the hill and Piercy Street, where I was born, is behind it.* To the right, across Great Ancoats Street, was Grange's corn shop [19] at the top of Store Street. *I used to buy my corn from there at one time. The Rose & Crown, a Groves & Whitnall house, was opposite on the corner of Store Street and Ancoats Lane.* Grange's building was still there in 1985 but it has since been replaced by new property.

Further along Great Ancoats

The former Ellesmere betting club, Warwick Street

Street, just before the canal, was Goolden's Buildings [20]. One of the old buildings was still standing in 1985, together with an arch and a gate which possibly once led to stables. *My mother used to send me here to buy candles and sometimes soap.*

Cross the canal and on the other side of the road on opposite corners of Chapel Street (now Chapeltown Street) were Nielsen Ladefoged's [21] and the Crown & Sceptre [22]. Both have now gone, but in 1985 they were still there: *The bacon firm is one of the few businesses there when I was a lad and still going today. The Crown & Sceptre was the pub where Crutchy Burns swept all the glasses off the bar. He lived in Long Street [now Longacre Street], which runs up the other side of the pub.*

On the left hand side of Great Ancoats Street is Pollard Street and as you look up it you can see John Hetherington's Vulcan Works [23] on the right, now split for different uses. Opposite the bottom of Pollard Street, a warehouse stands on the site of the row of shops [24] which Mick used a lot, where Myers Morris ran his boot repair business. On the corner of Epworth Street (formerly Wesley Street) is the site of the Wesley Hall [25]. *I went on day picnics from here and I lived at 8 Wesley Street at one time. There was a Groves & Whitnall pub at the Norton Street end kept by Ernie Knight and opposite was a yard and stables for horses, but it's all gone now.*

Continue along Great Ancoats Street until you can see down Every Street. *The houses on this side of the road were better quality than the ones in Wesley Street, that is they were lighter and had running water, though still no baths. As a child I lived in Tame Street, which ran parallel to Every Street, and later we lived in Every Street itself.* The Round House [26] was still there in 1985, with its windows bricked up. Here, Leslie Lever acted as the poor man's lawyer.

On the bend, as Great Ancoats Street sweeps round, was Ancoats Hall and the Horsfall Museum [27]. *The only official school trip I remember was to here. It was a beautiful place, but we had to write an essay about it afterwards! Later the building was used as a railway club when I was a member.*

Retrace your steps along Great Ancoats Street and turn left down Adair Street. *The Royal Mail Parcels Depot is where the Midland Railway Company's goods yard used to be. Nothing old is left on the street now but on the right hand side was the St Andrews Hotel [28], a Hardy's house on the corner of Norton Street. A bit further down at number 5 was Johnny Sands' tobacconist's [29] with its entrance into the back street which we used when we wanted to place a bet.*

The first turn left off Adair Street is St Andrews Square. Walk round the square. At [30] was Homer Street School and if you look through the gates into the Post Office yard you can still see the old sign for Arundel Street on the wall opposite. *This square is where the elite houses were and where Tod Sloan and Jack Sullivan lived. As you come back to Adair Street down the other side of the square you are walking along St Andrews Street, where Jim George's pub was. A walk down to the bottom of St Andrews Street will show you Helmet Street still there, but there is nothing of interest left on St Andrews Street itself. There was once a flight of steps from the square down to the park but they have been blocked off and are now on Post Office property. At one point I lived in Lelia Street, which ran parallel to St Andrews Street, between it and the railway.*

On the Travis Street corner of St Andrews Street is a stone cross [31], a reminder of St Andrew's Church which once stood in the square. The inscription beneath the cross has all but weathered away. It reads: "To the glory of God and in perpetual memory of the churchmen of this parish and congregation who gave their lives in the Great War 1914-1918 this cross and the tablet in the church are erected by their fellow churchmen."

Diagonally opposite in Travis Street was *Jim Lomas's pub, the Friendship* [32]. *Nearby was Henry Gittus' works [33] which made punching machines.* On the corner of Travis Street and St

55 Chapel Street, later Chapeltown Street. This was once the Railway Inn, known to all as Abigail's